Fear without loathing

Fear without loathing

Why life/work balance doesn't matter
but you do

Nicola Phillips

CAPSTONE

First published 2003 by
Capstone Publishing Limited (A Wiley Company)
8 Newtec Place
Magdalen Road
Oxford OX4 1RE
United Kingdom
www.capstoneideas.com

CIP catalogue records for this book are available from the British Library and the US Library of Congress

ISBN 1-84112-473-7

Designed and typeset by Baseline, Oxford, UK
Printed and bound by TJ International Ltd
This book is printed on acid-free paper

Substantial discounts on bulk quantities of Capstone books are available to corporations, professional associations and other organisations.

Please contact Capstone for more details on +44 (0)1865 798 623 or (fax) +44 (0)1865 240 941 or (e-mail) info@wiley-capstone.co.uk

contents...

For Lauren, of whom I am constantly in awe; with love, thanks and respect.

KT and LJ for truth, bizarromondo and them.

Vivian and Jonathan for corporate kundalini and body management.

Linda for keeping logistical shadows in their place.

Doe and Jed who both sneeze to their own different and creative dharmas.

Rich and Sade; I had to make my own music this time; do you think it helped?

Mark and Richard and the uniqueness of the people at Capstone. May it continue in the shadows...
Forget the lamppost...

Andy of the unique visual and temporal reality – may the time lords be merciful...

All of the people I have had the privilege to work with....
thank you.

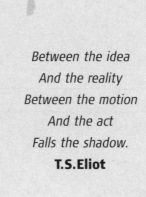

Between the idea
And the reality
Between the motion
And the act
Falls the shadow.
T.S.Eliot

This is a book about Fear. Fear lives in the shadow between idea and reality, the motion and the act.

One of the most over-used phrases of the moment is work/life balance. People are supposed to have a balance between their life and their work. This notion has become the subject of seminars, courses, dissertations and magazine articles. It doesn't seem to have changed anyone's life. In fact, it seems to have added to a growing list that people have of things they 'should' be doing – such as eating more lentils, going to kick-boxing classes, listening to people. Indeed, these lists seem to increase the stress that people already feel.

What people seem to miss is that all these things make it seem as though the solution to being happier at work and at home is 'out there'. It is down to some external factor such as working fewer hours, spending more time with the kids, going to a gym.

Wrong.

These are all about DOING.

Contentment, happiness, fulfillment, however you wish to describe it, is not about doing, it is about BEING.

You can DO a million and one new things, but if the thinking and feeling behind them is the same as your old processes, no change can occur. If it does, it will not be sustainable for any length of time.

You need to think differently in order to BE differently in order to have a more satisfying life.

So it is not about how many hours you spend at work or at home; it is about the way you think and feel in those places.

But why is it easier to DO rather than to BE?

Because we are frightened. Of what? Of what we don't know. Of things that are in the shadow.

You can't understand fear unless you learn how to be in the shadow.

Lurking in the shadow are many fears:
> **Fear of Beginning**
> **Fear of Fear**
> **Fear of Disappointment**
> **Fear of Success**
> **Fear of Choice**
> **Fear of Unworthiness**
> **Fear of Ending**

This book is about understanding what is behind the things you think and feel.

It is about understanding and relating to the fears we have that keep us stuck in places we don't want to be.

So what would I like to happen as a result of you reading this book?

In his book *Longitudes and Attitudes*, the New York Times journalist and author Thomas L.Friedman described the four reactions he wants his readers to have to his work. He wants them to read his columns and say:

I didn't know that

or

You know, I never looked at it that way before

or

You said exactly what I feel, but I didn't know how to express it

or

I hate everything you stand for.

I'd be happy with those responses, and I guess I'd add at least one more: It made me think about the way I am, and want to explore how to be differently.

This is a book dedicated to asking the questions and raising awareness about what it might be like to walk in the shadow with these fears, and why on earth you might want to go there. It's hard stuff, and is likely to be stuff you want to talk about or at least think and rethink. The book is meant to be the beginning of a thought process, so use it in that way.

Write the thoughts that occur to you as you feel them. It doesn't matter how stupid they sound. It's your book, your fears, do what you want.

Write in the margins.

Think in the margins.

The margins are between the thought, the reality and the shadow.

Let the margins draw out your shadows.

Do it in the margins...
Question.
Question me, you, anyone, anything that occurs to you.

Read it somewhere you wouldn't normally read it.
Re-read it.

Think about it.

'The best thing for being sad is to learn something... that is the only thing that never fails, the only thing which the mind can never exhaust, never alienate, never be tortured by, never fear or distrust and never dream of regretting.'

T.H. WHITE, *The Once and Future King*

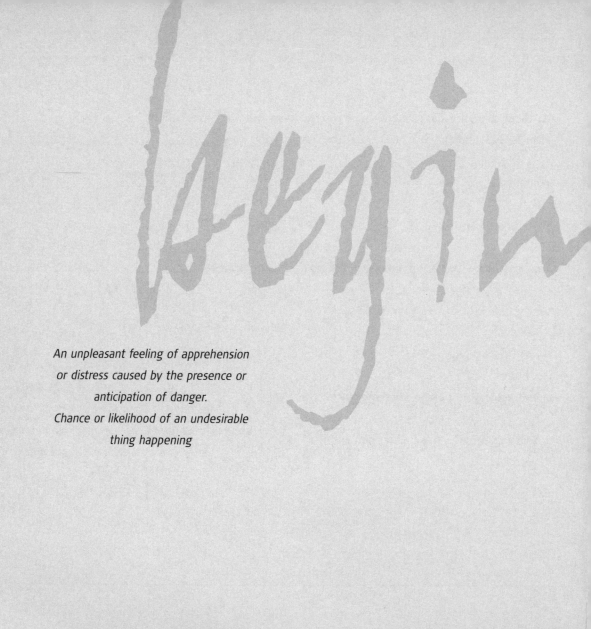

*An unpleasant feeling of apprehension
or distress caused by the presence or
anticipation of danger.
Chance or likelihood of an undesirable
thing happening*

fear of beginning

WHO MOVED MY KEYS?

Picture this scene:

It is night, and a passer-by is walking down a lamplit street. He stops at a lamppost, where he sees someone grovelling on the floor as if looking for something. He asks

>"Have you lost something? Is there anything I can do to help?"
>
>"I've lost my keys," replies the person.
>
>"Where were you when you last had them?"
>
>"I was over there," says the man, pointing over into the darkness beyond the lamppost.
>
>"So why are you looking over here?" asks the puzzled passer-by.
>
>"Because it's light over here...."

I bet you knew what he was going to say before you read it...

Why are we so frightened of the physical and metaphorical dark? Why is it that even when we know that we lost something in the dark, we won't go into the dark places to look for it, even though we know there is nothing to be gained by looking in the light?

Fear.

The other four letter 'f' word. The more unspoken of the two. Fear is the only four letter word not allowed in business. People find it harder to say fear than f***. Why? Why does it have a connotation of life and death when most of the things we fear are more everyday, happen to us everyday, and seem to be getting scarier? I guess we are as much afraid of life as death.

Why does it matter enough to write a book about it? Because fear is at the heart of pretty much every experience we have, whether pleasurable or otherwise. It can stop us doing things or inspire us to do things.

Do we greet it with pleasure? Hardly.
Do we invite it? Nah.
Do we manage it? Rarely.
Do we even acknowledge it?

I think that's the reason why we miss out on so much of life.

I think it's why we find so many issues, work and personal, to be insoluble.

I think it's why we find it hard to come up with creative solutions.

That's three good reasons why it's worth writing a book about it. So I have.
(Also it excited my publisher and he is never wrong.)

So, do you often get easily distracted from what you want to be doing?

Do you get easily tired?

Does everything you do feel as though it is not good enough?

Do you feel blocked and stuck?

Would you like to feel energetic, relaxed, alert and content with what you do?

Why can't you just do it?

It is a bit like the relationship between a writer and an editor. The editor criticises, and shapes the material that the writer generates. If the editor starts to judge the writer before they have seen the work, there is a problem. If a writer judges their work before they have created it, they get blocked.

If an individual is afraid that something will happen if they do something, they don't do anything.

In all of these cases the desire and freedom to move is paralysed by fear.

We are assaulted by the pulls and pushes of envy, desire, anger, greed, self-importance; but their root is fear.

We protect ourselves from fear and anxiety by distancing ourselves from it – in many different ways.

We do not suspend our judgements easily, neither do we have the unfettered capacity we had as children for curiosity and exploration. We lose them early in our lives through our need to manage the intrusive and different. As a result, many of us end up in unreal states, unaware of our bodies, ourselves, and unaware of being unaware.

So, dear reader, what you need is to accept and be with your fear; not lose it or conquer it, but be with it.

We need to learn to **respond** rather than react.

In order for us to cope with our fears of the world, we build ourselves up by our defences and then come to feel imprisoned by them. This leaves us feeling dissatisfied, irritable and cut off. In our attempts to be more self-assured, we tend to build up our defences even more, rather than disentangling ourselves from them. We try everything from coaching, external stimuli and therapy to finding something or someone to blame. This only exacerbates the problem and whilst it may make us feel temporarily better, it doesn't enable us to feel truer, happier or less fearful.

We imply that somewhere, out there, is an answer to our mystery of being, whether it is in a Zen monastery, a seat on the Board or a café in Rickmansworth.

Wrong. How can it be right? If it was, we would all have done it by now. The keys would be in the lamplight. Some of you will have tried it and found it wanting. People say that the answer is in plain sight, but it isn't. We keep it buried inside, because knowing that makes us responsible and culpable. There is no man behind the curtain, only ourselves.

Fear is about the white space between pictures. It is not about answers or gurus or self-help books. It's about confusion. It's about not knowing. It's about asking. It's about the space out of the lamplight. It's about the shadows.

It's about vulnerability. Accepting vulnerability is most of the way to accepting fear.

It isn't the fear itself that is harmful to us, it is the way we *react* to the fear that determines whether we grow or diminish.

So the quest becomes an acceptance of our fears.

So if it's the fear itself, how do you recognise it?
Recognising it and then acknowledging it is at least more than half the battle.

The other thing to bear in mind is that freeing yourself is nothing compared to the difficult task of knowing what to do with your freedom.
What would YOU want to be able to do?

A common, compelling film scenario is usually dependent on the characters wanting to do something but having something put in the way. The film then becomes the story of their reactions to, and how they overcome (or not), the obstacle(s).
What is it that you want to be able to do?
What is it you fear which is in your way?

Freedom usually begins with knowing what it is you want. (That is not the same as knowing what it is you DON'T want to happen.)
How do you know?

Like every quest, it means challenging many myths and assumptions.

Assumptions and connections. Question them all.

The fictions and myths with which we have populated our world may have some purpose or function, so before we terminate them in disgust, it is also worth examining how and why they came into being in that way. It is not about judging ourselves or what we have done; it is about knowing and owning ourselves. After all, when you get down to it, most of our being is based on various assumptions that we have accepted as true, however spurious the notion when you come to examine it closely.

Why is it that you cannot culturally question another's faith or religious beliefs, but you can question their political ones? How does one belief become an unquestionable?

In the same way we hold assumptions about ourselves that have become unquestionable.

"I've always been that way."   *How do you know?*

"That's just the way I am."   *How do you know?*

"That wouldn't work for me."   *How do you know?*

If your self-perception has never been questioned, if you have never let yourself challenge the basic assumptions you have of yourself, how would you know what really matters to you?

Evolution demands iteration, looping, branching and the creation of a feedback loop which informs your next stage. Understanding your assumptions about self is the beginning of your feedback loop. The output you get from this stage of your exploration becomes the input for the next. If you continue to use the same data you have been using and try to build a new you on top of that, you will always end up with the same you, maybe slightly adjusted.

To change the way you see the world, and react to it, you need to be clear about what governs your way of seeing the world.

You can't change your thinking with thinking – you have to feel something to change it.

You can't wash off blood with blood.
TIBETAN SAYING

You can't change your thinking with thinking.
You have to feel.
Many say face your fear; I say face your delusion.

Write down three key things that define you as a person.
Ask yourself what you do that demonstrates them.
(This may include things that you would perceive to be 'sacred' values to you.)

Write down three things that you fear the most.
Ask yourself what incidents you can recall which might have lead you to fear them.

The keys are in the dark, not under the lamppost.

So how do you begin? For hundreds of years people have walked El Camino. It's a spiritual pilgrimage route that goes from a village in France to another village in Spain. It's a walk that takes the average person six weeks. It isn't the length of the walk or even the scenery that attracts people. It's the spirit of doing it.

This book is not about the scenery or the fitness; it's about the spirit of doing it. The exhortation of this book is about living and being. You don't have to fall off a mountain or survive a disaster to feel alive. Being with your fears allows you to enjoy things without conditions. You can't enjoy with conditions; it is the lack of conditions that give us those inexplicable and usually indescribable moments of happiness in our lives. They are moments in the moment.

Being able to do this means not being afraid of your fears. Not worrying that at any moment, the pleasure might be taken away, or that you don't deserve it.

Fear does have a real purpose in our lives. It serves to warn us of genuine danger to survival. It is primal. It is not without cost that we fail to acknowledge fear. Fear is the key to many things and tells that that danger may be present. The importance of registering fear, and not hiding it or pretending it's not there, is essential for us to survive in a healthy way. If there is a stimulus one needs to register a response. It's like having your hand on the stove and not responding to the heat.

So it's important to know your fear and what your response to it needs to be; take your hand off the stove, or stay with the problem... It's about checking that the response is appropriate to the fear; so fearing that if you do not answer your mobile phone fast enough probably does not carry the same threat to life that a lion biting your rear might do. When you begin to challenge your assumptions about fears, you begin to realise that you don't know why you have kept this fear going. But you have to *begin*.

There is no way to begin other than to begin.

Reading and having insights is unlikely to be enough. Self-realisation is a long way from self-actualisation.. Learning how to take what you learn and apply it is as important as the insight itself. The 'so what' and 'what now' questions are essential. So read, say "a-ha" and keep asking the questions.

Keep asking questions. Keeping checking assumptions. Don't just do it once and think it's over. If not thought about, the knowledge gets stored in a filing cabinet somewhere. What a waste. Applying new knowledge always means risk and unfamiliar feelings. One of the reasons we look for answers is because vacuums mean the possibility of feelings. Answers are the refuge of the foolish and the faint hearted; so ye of little faith and no heart, do not enter here. Check your logical brain now.

Be ready to be uncomfortable, apprehensive, excited and surprised.

Growth means risk. No growth is possible without experiencing the unknown.

Be ready.

of beginning

fear

> Do not now seek the answers, that cannot be
> given you because you would not be able to live
> them. And the point is, to live everything. Live
> the questions now. Perhaps you will then
> gradually, without noticing it, live along some
> distant day into the answer.
>
> RAINER MARIA RILKE

THE KEYS ARE IN THE DARK.

The frightening things we do
sometimes, when we are afraid
to be afraid.

Dr PRAETORIUS, *People Will Talk*

fear of fear

The Buddhists speak of five fears:

Fear of loss of life

Fear of loss of livelihood

Fear of loss of reputation

Fear of unusual states of mind

Fear of speaking before an assembly.

Here is a more common one:

Am I the only teenager that masturbates?
ANONYMOUS

Fear itself is not something we actually label as something we do. We tend to be frightened, or feel defensive or confused. We are usually more familiar with the manifestations and symptoms of fear than with fear itself.

I think that comes from our need to feel that things have a purpose, a context.

If I go on and describe all of the known symptoms of fear, it is unlikely to mean anything to you, be of any help and would probably bore the pants off you. So what might be of value?

We tend to learn and understand by being able to put what we hear into a personal context:

How does this relate to me?

What experiences have I had that exemplify this?

What does fear mean to me?

Read this sentence again

I don't know whether a fear of loss of livelihood is more important to you than a fear of acting in a way that's different from everyone else. I am not sure that the comparative matters. What you need to be able to separate is the fear you have from the actions that you have as a result of it.

I'm not even sure we knowingly intend to hide our fears or our fear of fear. That doesn't mean that we don't do it, it just means we may not be aware of it.

So if this chapter feels more discursive and less focused than others, it is probably because it is. Sometimes starting anything is hard. Setting a context for self and others is hard. Why? I can only answer that question from my point of view. For me, it is a fear of not being able to express what I want to say in a way that a reader can identify with and feel something for.

In wanting to do something or be something, we frequently wake up our biggest fear; not being able to do it.

This chapter is about beginning to understanding one of the key manifestations of fear: Fear of fear.

What is the most common response we have to fear?
To defend against it, to DO something.

So in order to begin to understand what we are defending against, we need to look at the way in which we defend.

What would be the other end of the continuum?
To be able to BE with the fear, to let go and experience.

This isn't about doing. It's about being.

A friend rang me the other day and was talking about why it was so difficult for her to lose weight. I asked her why she wanted to lose weight, and she gave me all the stock answers about health, feeling better, etc. I asked her what effect her being overweight had on her environment. She thought for a while and said she didn't know. I asked her what it was that she wanted to feel differently by losing the weight and again she replied that she didn't know.

I also reminded her that she had recently succeeded in losing weight, not as a result of any newfangled diet but because her personal circumstances had changed, and instead of everyone telling her she should diet, she had done it because it was something she had wanted to do. She wanted to BE in a different way, not DO.

I don't think we think about how we want to BE differently in the world. I think all we think about is about what we want to DO differently.

If all we do is DO, then we change nothing about our state of mind.

Without a change in our state of mind, the actions may be different, but the thinking behind them is the same. Therefore, sooner or later, exactly the same patterns of behaviour and response are there, and we are left saying to ourselves that it is impossible for us to change anything; that's just who I am.

Well, it is just who you are, until you choose to think differently.

What stops you?

FEAR.
Fear of lots of things.
Fear of fear.

Where does it come from?
Why do we hang on to these dysfunctional ways of being?

When people talk of being frightened and unhappy, that is something they have in common with most of humanity. In our eagerness to eliminate fears and 'be real', we treat fears as something to be fixed and changed. We expect them to disappear when we have explained them. We distance ourselves from them and explain them away, frequently assigning blame for their existence on the past or the faults of others. We often describe them as a weakness, a character defect, a symptom of inadequacy.

They don't go away when we explain them.

How often have you said things like these to yourself?

"I can't do that because…"

"If only I was…"

"If only I wasn't…"

We are afraid to venture into the unknown because doing so reminds us how unsafe we feel or once felt. We don't like being reminded of being 'infinitely dropped'. Only when we stop fighting our fears can we appreciate that some form of transformation or even changed state is possible. Our way of thinking has been that if we can make ourselves stronger, the fear will go away.

Accepting the fear is what makes you stronger…

I believe that being able to be with the fear is what MAKES you stronger.

We need a way of being with the fear, so that we are not at risk of being overwhelmed by it. We are afraid to face the old sadnesses that live in our bodies and memories and often date from failures in the past. We hold on to them, are afraid to accept them and feel stuck. When you assess a situation with a rational mind and a fear of the dangers of the past resurfacing, you prevent yourself from having any kind of new and unanticipated experience. Nothing can change. In picking up this book, a piece of you is looking for a way to go more deeply into those painful places. The only way to go there is to go.

How often have you said "I just want to be somewhere I'm not"?

When I hear people say this, it seems important to talk about how they could have that experience and what is currently keeping them from having it. Sometimes when the desire seems so overwhelming, we think the only way to get there is by drugs, alcohol or some other external mechanism that allows us to be free of the bits of ourselves we don't like or are frightened of. Having someone tell you to stay with the pain sounds outrageously hard, but only by seeing the fear and accepting it does it become an acceptable part of us.

Only the person who can BE as well as DO has the capacity to feel real.

BEING not doing.
LETTING GO not defending.
It doesn't matter where you learn that from; it matters that you learn it.

Feelings aren't positive or negative. It's what we do with them that renders them constructive or destructive.

It's the same with fear.

So you can be afraid of the dark, but whether that then becomes something that affects your life is another story. Those two different things, the fear and your reaction to the fear, seem to become inextricably linked.

It is this linking which makes the fear so difficult to deal with – because we are not dealing with the fear, but with its effect. That means that we are forever treating the symptom without any hope of addressing the cause, so the problem becomes chronic.

The difference in attitude is between those who approach problems with their defences up and those who feel respect for the forces of nature and experience, and thereby have a heightened capacity to engage in complex issues. Defence means no inspiration; it's like being on board a spaceship that throws up its defensive shield whenever danger appears. It does this rationally to protect itself, but in doing so it stops many of its other functions, including the ability of the crew to override the shielding.

So should we fear more, not less?

Fearful – that is, full of fear – is not necessarily a bad place.

You can't ride a bike unless you give in to the fear. Without letting go, you fall off, or go over the handlebars. You only fall off when you hesitate or think too much.

Most people look for ways to 'improve' themselves, feeling that they have trouble letting go. They generally describe it as feeling out of control, or being afraid of losing control. They are blocked creatively or emotionally, are having trouble falling asleep or are having feelings of isolation and alienation. It seems to be more a fear of letting go. They seem to be looking for a way to feel more real, without realising that feeling more real means pushing self further into the unknown. Psychotherapy, through an examination of childhood, tends to turn people in a reflective direction, looking for the causes of unhappiness in order to break free from past sadness. Whilst this may indeed be helpful, it can degenerate into finding someone or something to blame for suffering.

The only way to stay in control is to let go.

It feels like we need to give some space in our minds for our fears, not to explain them away. This is letting go. It is the opposite of defending.

The patient is not cured by free-associating; he is cured when he can free-associate.
SANDOR FERENCZI

Creating a new environment where you can discover this capacity is the foundation to looking for the keys in the dark. It is about a new way to be with yourself and others.

Think about how you would describe your behaviour when you are anxious about something.

What would someone see you doing or saying?

If you don't know the answer to that question, then you need to find out...

If you do know, are you aware of what prompts you to act or speak in that particular way?

Are you aware of what it is in that particular circumstance that raises your anxiety and thereby your defences?

What is it that you are afraid might happen?

Questions, questions. When we are fearful, we rarely want questions. We usually want answers. What is it we fear about questions? Maybe we should ask what is so appealing about answers. The answer to that one is easy. Answers make us feel as though we are in control.

Control. In control. Out of control. The most common statements from people who are distressed:

"I need to feel more in control."
"I feel out of control."

For Stephen this means not having an item out of place in his wardrobe where everything is colour coded. His idea of disaster is when his partner has put his socks away and folded them incorrectly.

For Anna it means feeling unable to help friends through a difficult stage in their marriage. Feeling unskilled or helpless makes her feel out of control.

For Oliver, it means not having someone agree with him in an discussion. Not being able to make people think the same as he does creates a powerful force of anger.

When asked why they would be fearful of being out of control, they just repeated that they would not be in control. What is it that they fear about being out of control so much so that they don't want to be it?

There is no way to experience want, desire or fear without yielding control.

If you place two people in adjoining rooms, and expose both to intermittent loud noises, the person who has a button and believes pressing it decreases the likelihood of more noise is less anxious. Even people who have the button sometimes don't bother to press it, and their anxiety and tension levels are still low. What does this tell us?

The actual exercising of control is not critical. It is the *belief* that you have it that is essential. One example of this is that aeroplanes are much safer than cars, and yet more people are phobic about flying than driving. Why is this? Because despite the fact that we are more at risk in a car, most of us *believe* that we are 'good' drivers and are therefore more in control. In an aeroplane we have no control at all. It is the belief rather than the statistical hard data which governs our reaction to the fear.

Read it again – it does make sense, honestly...

If you can get your head around that, than try thinking about what you would need to believe to stop your fear damaging your ability to do something.

THE ONLY WAY TO BE IN CONTROL IS TO LET GO.

The Chinese expression for orgasm translates as 'having a high tide'. In a high tide, everything is floating, you are dissolved and there is no longer any foothold, but it does not feel like chaos. When you don't let your mind go, this floating becomes more like drowning, and then we start to panic. By doing that you doom yourself to a perpetual state of fear from which there seems no way out. You begin to tense yourself, to 'brace yourself', but all you get from that is tense shoulders.

Remember learning to float?
In order to swim, to stay afloat in the water, you have to let go and give yourself to the water. You cannot stay afloat otherwise. Floating demands letting go; there is water around you; believe it will hold you up, not suck you down… Floating is about being in the moment. When do we do it?

Have you ever given free reign to your imagination and noticed how quickly time passes when you do, how little fear you feel, how the only important thing is being in that moment?

Think of things which allow you to do that. Think of moments when you are so absorbed in the experience of the moment, that you neither want nor fear anything. It could be anything from a piece of music to seeing your child asleep in bed, to skiing downhill…

It's the small things that distract us and keep us frozen in time. These experiences come from the heart, not the head. We don't even need to process them, just be them.

Fear makes you think from your head, not heart. You can experience something in your head and heart. You remember it in your head, but what you draw from it in terms of growth is in your heart, not your head. The experience is in your heart, the memory and data from it in your head.

Sometimes that is why we sometimes seek absorbing or frightening experiences, like a roller-coaster, scuba diving or a bungee jump. When we have the time to think about things, they are no longer exciting and might even be scary. (Like the thrill of the chase in a new relationship.)

Trust life – if you're careful enough to listen, life does take care...
WAY OF THE GUN

So if we find it hard to be in the present, what do we do with the future?

One of the things we frequently defend against is the future and the unpredictability of life.

Either you are excited by life or you're not.
WATERLOO BRIDGE

In the film *Waterloo Bridge* the heroine believes that nothing good can happen or last. I could argue that she goes on to create a world in which this is true. Her fear *has* to come true or else the reality and safety of her world is shattered. The safety of thinking that we know what comes next is a big motivator. So we are perfectly capable of living lives which keep on replicating out worst fears, because then at least we can feel that we will know what comes next. Any deviation from this plot then becomes an unknown variable and we will strive to bring things back to the bad old days.

Fear breeds familiarity.

Things are easily spoiled when you want them to be.

THERE'S NO TIME LIKE THE PAST

It is the past, nothing more, nothing less. It is.
No one incident makes anyone who they are.
When you live in the moment you fear nothing. There is no fear. Nothing
matters except the moment – that's why zebras don't get ulcers.
There is no fear in the present. Fear only exists in the past and for the future.
The present is now and is happening; no time or place for fear.
Living in the present avoids the traps and distractions of the past and future.

Were we born afeared? Is it genetic? (I wonder what Stephen Pinker would say.)
I know it's a crucial part of survival, but the human species seem to have made
an art form of something that was originally very simple. It's why zebras don't
get ulcers. They keep fear for those occasions where it really is a matter of life
and death. We don't. We use it for anything from wearing the wrong clothes to
attacking an intruder.

Rosa shook her head. It seemed to be her destiny to live among men whose solutions were invariably more complicated or extreme than the problems they intended to solve.

MICHAEL CHABON, *The Amazing Adventures of Kavalier and Clay*

We do like to overcomplicate things down at the human waterhole. We seem to have created a reaction which is often disproportionate to the fear itself. Instead of saying "I have a fear, and it is of something that may be harmful to me, and should I need to help myself I will be able to do so", we say "I have a fear and I better protect myself because it is going to be really, really awful and it could happen any time and who knows whether I will be able to protect myself... Aargh!"

It's like contracting in childbirth; when the contractions are present the intensity is greater. When we contract in fear the pain becomes greater. When we learn to breathe through the pain, the pain doesn't go, it is still a part of us, *but it doesn't hurt so much.* It is also about separating the illusion and/or perception of fear from the fear itself.

Trying to avoid fear, even if you tried to think it through logically, makes no sense. How could you rationally explain how you could renounce any one aspect of an interdependent world, and not expect to hit it somewhere in your travels?

What happens to the fear if you feel it?

Is it gone?	NO
Calibrated?	NO
Risk assessed?	NO

It just is.

How do we know what our fears are and how they got there?
When we reach that place, how will we know what to do?
Those two questions are big enough to stop us embarking on such a serious journey.
What is the fear?
That we will fail?
All of the above?
What would help us?

So with all this background, I am hoping you are getting the picture that relieving your perceived stresses, feeling more happy or satisfied and being more rested, involves accepting your fear.

Rather than learning to accept our fears, our inclination is to run from them, and stay aloof from the feeling.

Most people that I work with as coach, counsellor or facilitator, are filled with rage, sadness or fear. On getting to know them I discover that they are completely unaware of what they are feeling. They can act their feelings out, but do not seem to know what they are. They frequently have little idea of what feelings are. They have no vocabulary for their feelings and emotions.

If you have no language with which to describe your feelings, does it mean they exist? If they are something you cannot describe having experienced, or may not even remember having them, does it make them less important?

Only when you are able to describe the feelings of fear can you develop the capacity to engage the feeling of fear, instead of experiencing physical or emotional sensations.

Most of the people I work with are also completely oblivious to the impact their behaviour has on others. It is usually this reaction from others that forces people to engage something other than a defence mechanism, although we are very adept at ignoring even the most blatant of messages from both others and our internal selves.

So how can you learn to describe fear?

Telling stories or listening to stories is another place to start. Case studies are pure facts and data (allegedly).When you read them you are expected to get something out of them. However, it is hard to get much personal meaning from them that transcends obvious content. They inform without enriching, as is unfortunately true of most learning in school. Factual knowledge only benefits the total personality when it is turned into 'personal knowledge'.

As children, we benefit more from fairy tales than true stories. As grown ups, many people internalise films, plays and songs better than they do facts. We seem to be more willing to accept them as long as they are not irrational. They have to appeal to both the rational and emotional before they are acceptable to us. Identifying with someone else's display of emotion is often easier to take than identifying with our own.

That is why many films and songs absorb you. What attracts you to them?

Write down a movie and a song that describes your greatest fear.
(If you write *The Life of Brian*, you need immediate help.)

Write down a movie or song that describes your ideal world.

Now try and describe the conditions for both your feared world and your ideal
world.

Hopefully the film or song helps you picture and then describe the things
which are important to you, those which are hard to describe in everyday
language.

So in the same way that some people believe that an illustrated story book
directs the child's imagination from how they, on their own, would see the
story and the characters, maybe on the other hand too much exposure to
visual depictions of story leaves people with the associations of the person who
made the pictures, not the individual themselves. We certainly find it easier to
have someone else imagine the scene of a story. But if we let an illustrator
determine our imagination, it becomes less our own, and not only does it have
no personal significance, but it may assume personal significance because it

exists. We therefore can end up believing that someone else's story is our own. This leads to immense difficulties when we try to work out the problems we have with what we perceive to be our stories when they are, in fact, the product of someone else's imagination. We may even be left with images of things that scare us, but which have no greater meaning or are of any importance to us as individuals. They belong to the individual who imagined them. In a similar way we become caught in other people's expectations of us. What we fear is not not meeting expectations, but the rejection that will follow if we don't meet the person's expectations.

That is the extreme end of being caught in a movie or song world. It isn't yours, it's someone else's, even if you have taken it as your own.

So what we need to do is to be able to do is:
■ Tell our own story as it is and was.
■ Understand our relationship and feelings to other people and situations in the story.
■ Be able to separate what feelings and responses belong to who we were in the past, and what belongs to us as individuals now.
■ Tell the story of what it is we want and seek

A story about describing fear:

Kathy was an extremely efficient manager. The trouble was, she drove everybody nuts while being efficient. People were not afraid of her, just very irritated by her abrupt manner. On telling her this, she replied "Well, that's just the way I am. I always get things done and there's a price you pay."

Was she happy with her behaviour?

What was she frightened of?

She was frightened of feeling. Frightened of enjoying herself. Frightened that if she did feel or enjoy, the work might not get done, and then she would have no way of being appreciated by others. Yet with her abrasive behaviour she had achieved exactly what she was frightened of; the lack of approval from others. So much for control...

When talking through her issues she would describe power struggles at work with just enough vagueness so that I could never be sure who was who or where the difficulty lay. Clarifying questions led to all sorts of passages and minor characters so that it was hard to know where to focus. It wasn't until I expressed the feelings of frustration that I had – I felt we were talking but not moving anywhere – that we were able to progress.

When I described this feeling, it seemed to release memories in Kathy. She described scenes of when she had been in hospital as a child. She had needed several serious operations which had left her in forced immobility in a hospital ward. Her frustration at being kept still in the bed at that time seemed to be still alive in her.

It seemed as though re-experiencing that feeling was too fearful for her to do on her own, to experience it again all by herself. Her desire to be 'superhuman' at work was part of a desire never to be 'sick', or out of control, again.

Her need to control extended to every part of her life including enjoyment. She only allowed herself to have 'fun' if she was doing things with a purpose. She related a story of how one day she found herself in a paper shop, and (she blushed as she related this) she found herself walking round the shop touching the different papers and delighting in the colours. She became very excited and bought lots of paper, but when she got home, she put the paper in a box, waiting for her to 'do something' with it. She could not bring herself to open the box and experience those feelings again in her controlled environment. Part of her really didn't want to do anything with it, but the part of her that did felt a lot safer.

Once she began to connect the feeling with the story, she became far less vague when talking about work. She went from 'I can't remember anything about my life', to small remembered facts such as where a particular box used to sit in her bedroom as a child. She became much more tolerant of her frustration at work and of her colleagues, even when she felt unsupported by her boss.

These situations lost some of their force when she realised how vulnerable and how fearful she was in any kind of frustrating circumstance. She had appreciated that she needed to separate the fears of Kathy the child from the fears of Kathy the grown up. She was a different person now; those fears were appropriate for the child then, but not for Kathy now. She could allow herself to feel the excitement without the fear, but she had to experience the fear first. She described it as two different sides to her. Integrating the two was the key. (But she had to go into the shadows to find the key...)

Rather than acting her fears out, she learned how to feel them.

What would you say to Kathy?

Fear means knowing your personal doubts. When you pretend it doesn't exist, you lose all of the things it can teach you. When you let go of fear, it disperses itself. Name it and accept it.

Doing it is not the fearful part; thinking about it is.

So stop thinking about it and do it. It's less frightening.

In the moment you have no time for fear.

Let's come back to the present.

Most of the time the present is virtually non-existent for us. We are so consumed by using the past to plan what comes next, a moment away or in the future.

How hard is it to be there? Being still and just observing what is going on around you is so hard. It takes enormous effort just to be there. Try it. See how long you can listen to yourself being and what is going on around you. Listen to everything; cars going by, your breathing, the fridge switching on and off... I would be surprised if you can do that for longer than two minutes; usually after about a minute, we begin to think. Our interest in just being with reality is very low. We want to think through all of our preoccupations and figure life out. So before you know it, you have forgotten about this moment, and have drifted off into thinking about your house, personal relationships, children, boss, etc. Nothing wrong with it except in doing that we have lost something else. The something else is the ability to be in our reality.

We do this most of the time... and we do it because... well, usually we are trying to protect ourselves from something. Yes we spend a whole lot of time defending ourselves against something that has either already happened or we are actually powerless to stop. When we are defending we have no concept of reality, because the defence blocks it. In fact, it frequently is denying reality's existence, because if we deny its existence, we don't have to do anything about it.

There is nothing wrong with considering current problems and/or planning ahead. However, when we are upset or stressed about an issue, we don't just plan, we obsess. Not knowing what to do sends us into an even more anxious state. If this continues over a period of time we often become physically or mentally depressed. If our mind is refusing to take care of a situation then our body takes over. At this point, we catch a cold, get skin rashes or recurrences of old viruses.

It is unlikely that we could ever stop this happening completely, as sometimes our worry is so strong that it blocks everything and it takes a body shock for us to recognise what is going on. Also, our defences can be so strong that we think we can carry on through something and if we focus hard enough, it (that is, the worry) will go away.

So we return once more to the centre for most of these stuck patterns of behaviour: this flawed desire to control what happens because of fear of fear. Flawed, because you can't.

Controlling doesn't let you do what you'd rather be doing.

It merely stops what you perceive to be bad things from happening.

It rarely creates or inspires.

The other problem with trying to control things is that exerting control over one thing inevitably impacts on another. There is an Abenaki Indian story about a young warrior who was very frustrated by the fact that every time he tried to paddle across the river the wind kept pushing him back. He decided he would have to get the wind under control and so went in search of the source of the wind. After a long search, he found it high in the mountains in the form of a wind eagle who he called Grandfather. He tricked Grandfather into falling into a crevice between two mountains and by taking the wind out of the world took all the movement out of the world. The weather got hot, the ponds dried up and filled with rubbish, the fish and animals died and the people were miserable. Stopping the wind made everyone uncomfortable. In the Tibetan medical system 'wind' is used as metaphor for mind, because they are both in constant motion. Anyone who has any kind of what we would call emotional disturbance is said to have a 'wind disorder'. Trying to calm the wind or tame it into submission means a tension of the mind and frustration. Not only does

Pulling on a thread in one part of the system always affects another part somehow.

the wind have a purpose, frustrating though it might be sometimes, but not having it creates a gap in the larger system of things. We need the motion to move and grow.

We tend to either assume control or hand over control; often a mixture of the two. Of course the irony is that the tighter you hold on, the less control you have. If you feel the need to hold on you are effectively saying that there is something out there which has more control than I do, so I had better hold on so that they can't control me. See the paradox? The only way to be in control is to let go. Be with the fear.

Sometimes behaviours begin as coping mechanisms or rituals which were necessary to help us survive or work through something.

Everyone has history. Everyone has difficulties from their past. The way we express them in the present may govern our ability to move away from them.

When frightened, we tend to freeze up. We lock ourselves up physically. (Yup, we still want to stay in control; we haven't really let go in our hearts and our heads.) When we are relaxed, we walk freely and our arms swing in opposition to each other. When we are afraid, our arms go to our sides and when asked to swing them or relax, we stiffen up completely. We rarely know this and when someone tells us, the instinctive response is to deny it, as we are full of fear. The isolation of fear means we don't move in relation to space or people, whether that is a physical or a psychological move.

Letting go means accepting the energy that you are getting from the outside world.

Don't just do something; sit there.
THICH NHAT HANH

You cannot learn something new until you have emptied yourself. There is a famous story about a Zen master who was visited by a professor who wanted to learn about Zen. The master served the tea. He poured his visitor's cup full, and then kept on pouring. The professor watched the overflow until he could bear it no longer. "It is overfull. No more will go in."

"Like this cup," the master said, "you are full of your own opinions and speculations. How can I show you Zen unless you first empty your cup?"

Our cup is usually filled to the brim with the 'obvious', 'common sense' and the 'self-evident'.

In order to move, we have to first yield, empty, and then push forward. Pushing before yielding and emptying results in pain and blockage.

Y	Yield	*accept your fear*
E	Empty	*let go*
P	Push	*follow your intuition*

Michelle Miotto suggests that unless you yield your body, the energy cannot flow. Try it. Stand up and breathe in. Breathe out and feel your shoulders drop. You may even be able to feel how tense you are. Be conscious of it and then give in to it. Feel the weight of your body moving from your muscles to your bones (that is, from a place where they are tense, to the place that was meant to hold your weight). Don't fight it. Yield on your life's push. You only begin to feel what is when you yield. As you begin to yield you feel the resistance, that is part of you. You need to feel the resistance before you can empty it.

Yield.
Yield and accept what is.

Yield is about accepting possibilities.

Think about it.
Don't keep pouring.
Try not to just rush to the next paragraph. Let the implications sink in.
Yield.

You cannot empty until you yield.

When they think they know the answers,
people are difficult to guide.
When they know that they don't know,
People can find their own way.
LAO-TZU, *Tao Te Ching*

What don't you know?

The 'don't know' mind is important to being there. If you 'know' a place or a person, you pass through it or by them without looking.

So, what does yield look like? Try this exercise to see how willing you are to yield.

Try counting to five without thinking of anything, and as soon as you think of something, go back to one. If you can actually do it, try counting to ten. It is an extraordinarily hard thing to do, particularly when you are being challenged by a person to do something. That should be a clue as to things that might stop you emptying: doing things in response to a challenge, or force, makes it hard for you to let go. You already have a competitive aim and expectation in your head. That is not empty.

Back to one. This is a hard thing to do. Because you can't do it immediately, don't give up. Many people take years to be able to count to ten in this way. Knowing that you can't do it overnight should be a relief not a pressure. Yielding means being more aware of what you do and what your environment does. If you have a plan in mind, you see things in terms of that plan, not as they are.

A plan is a list of things that don't happen.
WAY OF THE GUN

Back to one. The more you try to overcome your thoughts intruding, the more you do. To free yourself from the need to get results, you need to know what the 'one' is for you. If you don't know where you are, or what is important, you have no way of knowing how you are doing in getting there. You have to yield and empty before you can move on. To start by trying to make things happen is meaningless.

Heading straight for a list of actions to do will give you at best, a list of things you have done, but no sense of achievement. Hence the emptiness many stressed people describe, and yet they are busy all the time...
They are not empty, they are actually full...
Their Zen cup is overflowing. They cannot take anymore in; yet the cup is so busy overflowing that they can't drink from it. So they think their lives are full, but they cannot drink from their overflowing cup.
New skin does not flourish until the old has been sloughed off.

When the Zen master kept pouring tea into the professor's cup, he was trying to shock him into a new way of seeing himself. He wanted him to tune into the empty space of his mind rather than identify only with its contents. Identifying with the contents continues to reinforce reactions to fear rather than feeling the fear.

Empty.

Empty is not ignorant. It is open to new.

How often have you slept on something to discover that the solution has appeared to you in the night? Sleep allows your 'don't know mind' to come to the fore; usually when you are not thinking about the things for which you want solutions.

It's like learning to ride a bicycle. You begin by getting on the bike, pushing on the pedals and falling. You try and fall several times, but find it hard to balance yourself. Suddenly, for no apparent reason, you achieve equilibrium and are riding the bicycle. It isn't the result of countless tries, but happens only when you allow the bicycle 'to ride you'. You accept the lack of balance between the two wheels as a way of being, and then instinctively, intuitively, without conscious logical thought, convert the initial force towards falling into a greater force on the pedal. You don't think this through as a rational process and can only work out what has happened afterwards, but it is the letting go that puts you in control.

Using an opponent's force to increase your own is at the heart of aikido practice.

Let the fear ride you.

Don't take an explanation in place of an experience.
Don't try and understand what you are feeling, just feel it.
Pay attention to everything exactly as it happens, and DON'T JUDGE IT.
Breathing happens on its own.
Let the breath breathe *you*.
Fear happens on its own.
Let the fear feel *you*.

In order to be with and tolerate the fear, you have to accept the fear and also feel that there is something else you can do; some other way of being other than thinking. Telling you to let go is not enough; you will need something to do with your mind to get it out of the way.

How can you get your head out of the way so that you can have your experience in peace?

Sometimes people with a psychological stammer are taught to distract themselves when a stammer is imminent by lightly stamping their feet, or touching something near to them. By doing something with their minds they allow enough space for the words to come. This works with people who have an anticipation, or fear, of what will happen when they speak, so it prevents them getting the words out. In order to get the words out they need to get their minds away from anticipating and initially into a form of distraction. Once the fear becomes diminished, the distraction is no longer necessary, as a new experience has been created.

You need to learn how to get out of your own way so you can be with the experience you need to be with.

Sometimes it pays to speak without thinking in a safe environment. The scary thing is how much we don't. How much we protect ourselves and what we say and do. Sometimes we discover what we need to say when we get out of the way of ourselves.
What would be your new experience, and your new setting?
You need to be able to lose yourself without feeling lost.

It is not about just changing your actions or even the thoughts behind your actions; it is about changing the model that created them in the first place. Keep asking the questions, never be content with your first response. Keep asking why:

R I can't tell my boss about this problem.

Q *What is it you can't tell him about?*

R My problem – that I don't think the job is do-able in the time he has requested.

Q *What is it that concerns you about his response?*

R Nothing concerns me; I just don't want to look stupid.

Q *It sounds as though something does concern you. How do you think he will respond?*

R He is going to be mad at me.

Q *What would make him mad at you?*

R Not doing as he asked.

Q *So why does that concern you?*

R Because… I don't know, I don't want him mad at me!

Q *What leads you to believe that he will be mad at you?*

R I just know.

Q *What is it he has done or said that leads you to that conclusion?*

R I just know.

Q *I get the impression that you have come to a conclusion, and have a fear and expectation about what will happen, and are now convinced that that is the only possible outcome.*

R   That is correct.

Q   *If that is true, and there is only one possible outcome, why are*
           you still so anxious if it is inevitable?

When you are locked into a single intent, it is impossible to see any other way.
Q is standing in the shadows asking the questions. You need to be Q to your
own R. You need to check your own irrational logic. (You may get lucky and
find someone else to do it for you. It really helps.)

*Now try reading the
questions again...*

Oh, and the last one (there were three parts: **Yield**, **Empty** and ...**Push**).

Push.

This one is easy. This is the one you have been looking for. The one you don't
need help with. The doing one. Follow your intuition. Let go and don't defend.

That's it. Once you have accepted, emptied and let go, it's easy (and dead exciting).

- Its not the feeling of fear that inhibits growth; it's the way you respond to the feeling that renders it constructive or destructive. YOU choose.

- The more you defend against a fear, the bigger it becomes, and your perceived need to defend against it.

- Trying to control an irrational feeling such as fear by using rational thought is like trying to put out a fire with oil (totally irrational).

- Fear and desire are so closely linked that when you defend against one you inevitably defend against the other, and therefore defend yourself from the truth you are.

FEAR MORE, NOT LESS.

Our defence mechanisms come into play only when we feel we are being attacked, however often or real that may or may not be. They have no life or reality of their own. We create their existence, and thereby our own isolation. When we learn to leave the defences alone we appreciate that they have no durability, or indeed viability, unless we give it to them.

That is where our control lies; in learning to be with the fear, and not the defence.

of fear

Follow the fear
DEL CLOSE

The place you are most fearful of is the place you probably need to be.

Don't cling to the lamppost.
Stand in the shadows.
The keys are there.

disappoi

"Supposing a tree fell down, Pooh,
when we were underneath it?"
"Supposing it didn't," said Pooh after
careful thought.
Piglet was comforted by this...
A.A.MILNE, *The House at Pooh Corner*

fear of disappointment

When your light is my shadow...

Would that we could all be as comforted as quickly as Piglet.

Fear of being special.
Fear of not being special.
Fear of not being perfect, played out by driving for perfection.
Fear of missing out.

"We have paid a terrible price for civilization. We are all in states of depression because we cut ourselves off from many of the impulses because we are terrified of what we might do. We think we are much worse than we really are, and put ourselves into terrible states of control that we call civilization, and that makes us very unhappy. It is time to turn over the stone and see whether what's underneath is really so terrible."
DECLAN DONNELLAN

That is how one man sees the world, but it does raise the question of how bad things really are. Maybe life is not all pain or trouble, but we do have an inordinate fear of things not going as planned or as we expected.

Have you ever painted an extremely black picture of a situation, way blacker than it merited?
Do you often see the glass of life as half empty?
Do you worry about things being 'not quite right'?

If you answered yes to all or any of the above, you too have a fear of disappointment.

We have all been disappointed in our lives. It is probable that we will be so again. Yet we still fear the inevitable. Why?

Fritz Perls suggested that everything is a projection. If a person is scared of disappointment, they have probably been disappointed. Because we are often scared of life's grand and uncertain adventure, we begin to think that we are wise and smart to ask for very little. We hear the sounds from the confusion room of the unknown, and convince ourselves that rather than experience that, we should stay where we are (and then bitch about how boring life is).

We fear disappointment and the chaos of a potentially disorganized future, and believe we can avoid it by not admitting that it's a possibility.

We stay fixated in the same pattern of behaviour because it's what we are used to doing, even though it takes us nowhere and makes us feel confused. However, at least we will be familiar with it – and we won't be disappointed or disappointing.

We cease to ask for anything more than we are prepared to give. If we truly believed this, we would feel happy staying there. But we rarely are.

The fear of disappointment unfortunately doesn't stop with us. We have a nasty habit of projecting our half-empty glass on anyone who comes close to our defence mechanisms. We often project our resentment and disappointment out to others; we become cruel to others or situations around us, and eventually to ourselves. This creates the myriad of neuroses and obsessions to protect from the pain of what we have created for ourselves.

It seems such a crazy notion to always think that bad things will happen, that it's worth telling some stories of disappointment to illustrate the varying ways this fear presents in our lives.

Three stories of disappointment

MARK HAD A HISTORY OF FORMING RELATIONSHIPS, both personal and professional, which had a very clear pattern to them. They began as relationships of total and utter commitment; in personal terms this meant deep and passionate attraction and sometimes devotion. In professional terms, it meant seeing a job or a boss in the job as the answer to everything. The 'best thing that could/had ever happened' to him; this was it. He invested all his emotion in the 'other', whether it was a person or job.

Unsurprisingly, his relationships would begin as 'this is the one' and always end up with him running away from them, usually blaming the other person. His jobs would begin as 'I've finally found what I've been searching for', and end up with him leaving, blaming his boss and the company culture for not understanding him.

In both cases, Mark stopped idealizing both his partner and the job the way he once had, because it made him too insecure to adore someone who could be so disappointing. His fear of being disappointed led him to be disappointed, every time. Unfortunately, his experience of disappointment – that he himself had created – led him to be even more vicious about people. The only way he felt he could exist in a world of such potential disappointment was by making everybody he came into contact with 'bad'. He would undermine and belittle people in public, both in his personal and professional life, to the point where he has no respect from work colleagues and finds it hard to find people to go to the pub with.

It is not his fear of disappointment, but his reaction to that fear, his perceived defence against it, which has led him to a very lonely place.

"I NEVER DESERVED TO BE IN THE AUDITION in the first place." Carol was very used to feeling unworthy. When the job she had been waiting three months for – and which she had been told was in her pocket – became the victim of corporate politics, she immediately felt very angry that she had let her defences down and begun really wanting the job. She had exposed this vulnerability, and in fact it was probably part of her original success with the people who interviewed her that she was honest and excited. At the beginning she kept her defences high to protect her from disappointment and of disappointing others. As it looked more positive, she became more confident as she felt there had been no hiding of her warts, and no one was expecting things of her which she couldn't fulfil. At the last fence, a new candidate entered the ring with more experience than she had, and soon the old defence pattern of 'well, I was never worthy in the first place' re-asserted itself to become herself.

SIMON WAS DESCRIBED BY HIS WIFE as someone who was easily manipulated by other people who had a stronger will. He had no sense of direction, and was easily swayed. He himself was terrified that he would disappoint not only her, but their children.

Read that again, it's important

He actually did know what he wanted; not to disappoint anyone. The problem was that this is a negative wish, which usually means a fear not a desire, so you always end up defending against it rather than seeking it.

Ask yourself whether your dreams are in fact fears.

In Simon's case, he loved so much that the reach of his heart exceeded his finite capacity to make everyone happy. (It would exceed most people's.) He would experience an impossible feeling of wanting to be in several places at once, feeling pulled in different directions, wanting to make everyone happy; even feeling that he could make everyone happy – if only they would cooperate and somehow not need it all at once. If only...

There seems to be nothing wrong with Simon's desire to love, but it can only operate in the world he has constructed. This is only a problem when it conflicts with the world his wife and children have constructed. Unless he can see that, he is perpetuating a situation whereby he is doomed to keep living his greatest fear of disappointment.

"We women adore failures. They lean on us."
OSCAR WILDE, *A woman of no importance*

The common denominator in these stories is a fear of what another individual might do to the person at the centre of the story. Fear of being seen as the perpetrator. The one who did the harm. The one who persecuted. Who didn't rescue. Victims will do anything not to be seen at the perpetrator, as that might render them responsible in some way.

The one who is disappointed or who disappoints.

It is about needing to get past the clinging: whether it is to a person or thing; about creating space for yourself without a dependency on others – as their rescuer or persecutor.

How do you create the space for yourself when you are used to creating the space for someone else, or to someone else creating it for you?

A parent needs to discover how to create an environment that nourishes the child without over-feeding. Over-anxious parents frequently create children who feel mobilised to respond to their parents' anxiety; they become too attentive to others, and afraid of their own depths. They cannot have their own experience.

Jung suggests that whenever the parent leaves the child, the child suffers a 'little death.' Getting used to this is part of a child's normal development. If they don't appreciate the ability to be on their own, as opposed to being alone, their fear develops into an obsession and/or phobia. If the parent always stayed with the child, the child would suffer the delusion of safety because they were not integrated into the world. Their fear has not been taken away by the parents staying; in fact it becomes greater, the more used you are to it. The more habituated we are to things and people, the harder it becomes for us to let go; we fear we have more to lose. Once again, creating the illusion of safety increases the fear that we already have: that it will be taken away. And yes, we have increased that fear ourselves.

This inability to be alone, or with yourself, prevents you from being able to explore your internal self and fears. It increases the shadows.

You have to feel able to be in a room with someone else, but not compelled to do anything for them, be anything for them and trust that they will not intrude on you. That is a very tough call, and if you have no experience of it, it is hard to make sense of it, or what it might look like.

Should I stay or should I go...?

I know I am saying it again, but understanding fear is not like learning how to make a presentation. It involves being in unknown and therefore uncomfortable territory. Also if your universe is defined by doing, than it is very hard to imagine what being would look like. It's like a good coach who needs to be present but uninterfering. They need to be there to guide, to let you have your experience, but not to be depended upon.

Do you have a friend whom you have to say very little to, but you still feel good in their presence? You allow that person to be with you without even necessarily interacting. They are in the room, without you needing anything from them, or needing to do anything for them.

It's a bit like the feeling you may sometimes experience just before you go to sleep, when you are aware of the basic patterns and noises around you – light, snores, voices – and no anxiety or fear about what they hold for you. You just let them wash over you. What would you need to put in or take out of your current environment to experience that feeling?

So being able to experience that feeling of neither disappointing nor disappointment, an ability to be with others without needing to intervene or be intervened with, is one way of being with the fear.

This is one side of the coin; the other side of this fear is a desire for perfection that you perceive is the only thing that will keep you from disappointing others.

MARK EPSTEIN TELLS A STORY of his moment of realisation about when he learned to be with his fear of disappointing; his need for perfection.

Mark had spent a great deal of time looking at the way he interacted with people and what created the very different relationships he had with others. He really felt he was getting somewhere, and went away and spent a week on a meditational retreat to give him the opportunity to let go of issues and just to be with his feelings. At the end of the retreat he felt a great sense of enlightenment; that everything had changed, but nothing had altered. Feeling very 'quiet' from ten days of meditation and seeing his thoughts in glorious Technicolor, he proceeded to lock himself out of his car as he was leaving.

His keys were definitely under the lamppost; in the car. He could see them. He felt terribly foolish, and concerned about how he would be seen by people at the meditation center. So proud of his achievements, so aware, and yet he locks himself out of the car. He had felt himself so confident when he had got ready to leave that morning, and now he was panicking; wondering what good all that practice had done if he could do something as stupid as lock himself out.

He was disappointed that the retreat had not yielded a more efficient self. After a few minutes of thought, he realised that he was not humiliated, just embarrassed. He did not allow his thoughts to go over and over the event endlessly. He called for an AA man to help him, and while waiting began to adjust to his reality:

He did not need to be perfect or infallible to get home.

He did not need to always be in control.

He did not need to be perfect.

The retreat had changed something in his way of thinking. Instead of his usual contraction and self-punishment, he actually felt a spirit of generosity towards himself. He did not have to be perfect to be OK.

He was enough.

I realized that my awareness was now stronger than my neurosis ... I did not have to let my identity as an efficient and together person imprison me.
MARK EPSTEIN

We seem to have a need to do everything, have everything, be everything.

Compulsions

Addictions

Obsessions

Fear of not being perfect.

The opposite of the unknown. The familiar.

Fear of not being perfect is one of the most powerful blocks. It brings us face to face with our judging spectre, and since we can't possibly measure up (to standards *we* have set) we procrastinate. We envision how something or someone has to be perfect, and then when we are disappointed that they fail, we withdraw. This withdrawal is usually accompanied by a sense of general unhappiness with the way things are. We generate fantasies of how wonderful and horrible everyone else is, fantasies of omnipotence or their inverse, victim or bad luck fantasies.

Another view of the half-empty glass.

We even try to make disasters perfect.

When you are in the grip of fear, there are no half measures, no logic, no rationale. In this situation, you move from something not being quite as you expected, to the world having fallen apart.

One brick out of the house, the house falls down; I haven't just lost my keys, somebody has already found them, crashed my car, and burgled my house.

Being with the fear demands a level of being able to see and describe what is happening as opposed to your worst nightmare. Your worst nightmare may not be your fear, just an extreme version of it.

When you appreciate that you can never have what you think you deserve, you will be able to relax. You stop feeling deprived and empty when you stop taking it personally.

Symptoms usually contain a hint of their own cure. Usually we have created a pattern of making ourselves, for example, unapproachable by wondering obsessively whether people like us or not. Only by distracting yourself from those thoughts will you learn what it would mean to be there for someone. We fear what we most desire, that letting go of self that accompanies a powerful connection – where we forget ourselves and are enriched by another (or something). But we restrict the capacity we have to make this happen. We yearn for the kind of connection our own thinking protects us from. In a kind of compulsive way, our repetitive thinking, our known patterns of being – for example the way we go to work, our rituals at work, working itself – squeeze the life out of life.

That should wake you up.

It's not always about you...

The old ego dies hard, such as it was, a minister of dullness, it was also an agent of security.
SAMUEL BECKETT

We all take such pains to over-educate ourselves. In the wild struggle for existence, we want to have something that endures, and so fill our minds with rubbish and facts, in the silly hope of keeping our place.
OSCAR WILDE, *The Picture of Dorian Gray*

How often have you substituted knowledge for wisdom, confused facts with answers?

The sense of beatitude had passed. Reason took its place, and my fear of the unknown, along with an urgent need to get my feet back on the ground, had returned.
PAULO COELHO

Why is it so important to keep your feet on the ground?
Why do we run to reason instead of accepting what appears to us instinctively?

It is quite a revelation to appreciate just how much of our thinking is repetitive, closed and pointless. It keeps you isolated and cut off from the things you value most. Have you ever asked yourself "I wonder, if I put as much time into experiencing my life as I do worrying about it, whether I would get more done"?

If you haven't, ask yourself, and ask yourself what things in particular YOU obsess about?

Martin was clearing out his house as he prepared to move. He found he had many insurance policies; many more than he needed. In fact, most of them were duplicate policies. He said he had bought them just in case. I asked him just in case of what, and he said in case there was something wrong with the original one. When he added up this manifestation of his need for safety, he found that he could cash in about £8,000 worth of policies. And, guess what, it didn't make him any safer. What he was insuring himself against, or was trying to, was unpredictability. Although his rational self told him that there was less than no point and he was actually wasting his money, his irrational, fearful self was saying "well, just in case… you never know…"

His need to control his environment came from a fear of not doing it right. The most prominent figure in his life was his grandmother, who had been a very strong parent to him. She was highly principled, with a strong and consistent sense of tolerance and fairness.

He would describe himself as wanting to be the same way. Yet in his dealings with people at work, he could not help but be judgmental if they did not appear to be doing things the way he wanted them to.

He so wanted to be like the role model he aspired to, but was so frightened of him disappointing his role model, (and himself), that he set up two major defences:

- Planning everything and not wanting to do anything that wasn't planned. This also involved never being in the moment as he never knew what might happen next if he stopped to enjoy the moment. And of course, if he didn't know what was going to happen, then he might not be ready or do the right thing...
- Judging everyone else as not able to do the job as well as he could. In reality, he did trust most of them, but in order to protect himself against any perceived hostility, he had to 'make' them hostile to him in his irrational mind, so they could be 'bad', and he could be 'good': that is, know better.

I know these behaviours sound daft, but most people have convoluted defence mechanisms that have evolved over the years to protect them from their worst fears. When we are faced with them, we become almost ashamed of how daft they are. In our irrational heads and in the name of protection, nothing is ever too much, or too silly.

How daft and silly are yours?

Martin has a huge fear of not doing it right every time. It has stopped him being in the moment, and prevented him from enjoying what he does, both personal and professional. His wife told him that when he proposed he told her not to get excited as they weren't married yet, and when she said she was pregnant, he said "don't get excited, we haven't had the baby yet."

It has taken a while for him to appreciate that he will need to let go of his defences if he wants to enjoy life. Letting go of something that has been around for over thirty years is difficult, and it has been important for him to feel that there was another way of doing things when he let go of the old one. Now he is buying a house which is impractical in many ways but he *wants* to do it. Instead of doing what he feels he ought to, he has chosen to do what he wants.

He still looks for approval:

M: I think I react very differently now, and am less sensitive to personal stuff – well, I think I am.(Raises eyes and looks at me.)

N: What were you thinking about when you looked at me?

M: Don't know. (Long pause.) I suppose I wanted your approval.

N: I'm not sure what you mean by my approval. Even if I told you that I thought you were doing the right thing, it would not let you relax. What could I say that would truly make you feel you had done the right thing and relax and feel confident?

M: (After pause for thought.) Actually, I'm not sure anything would convince me. It might temporarily do something, but I suppose it wouldn't make me feel safe.

N: No point in my doing it then.

M: *gives the smirk of the found out...*

So let's get really heavy and talk about the ultimate disappointment.

Difficulty, disappointment and failure are necessary pieces of our lives. We learn from them, or should do. Hiding or denying them does not make them go away, neither does a desire for them not to exist. Developing a way of thinking that accepts and takes no position allows us to learn from them.

One teacher recommends pretending that you are dying and there is nothing you can do. The only inevitability we occasionally allow is the inevitability of mortality, and then often unknowingly. When you really accept there is nothing you can do, and stop judging, you stop reacting and begin to live.

For example, it is usually harder for a carer to bear pain than a victim. It is hard to watch someone else suffer, but when you know that that is your only choice, you accept it. For the victim you know you have it, and you have to deal with it. The fact that someone else is suffering should not be an invitation for you to do the same. You cannot cure everything or stop all pain.

At the top of the tragedy list is the ultimate tragedy, death. It is more tragic for those around than for the person experiencing it.

The people farthest away from tragedy and trauma are the ones who are more disturbed; the children of holocaust survivors, Americans who were not in New York City for 9/11. We even encourage that by only being interested in the victims of disaster, not the survivors. The victims know what they have to deal with, the observers almost wish they did. In a very perverse way, they wish they were going through it and then at least people would look after them, and they would not feel the stress and responsibility for another. It is so much easier to be a victim, perceived or real.

For genuine victims, it is easier to choose to be with the fear. If you know there is nothing you can do, all expectation and guilt is taken away. One of the reasons why hospice workers enjoy their work is because their clients know what their purpose is and often are with the moment, without expectation, in the knowledge and acceptance that they will die soon. That's a big relief.

On a lighter scale if you can accept what is genuinely, you automatically begin to relax.

Buddhists believe that death is the source of enlightenment, so they do not fear death. They believe that all life, and its practice, is a preparation for death. The time before death, of death, and after death are all opportunities for enlightenment. Buddhist monks were asked to teach the Samurai warriors how to be in a state of equilibrium when they went into battle; to be able to experience fear and not let it impact on their ability to fight successfully. In effect, it was about being with their fear in order to increase their energy, not to deplete it.

Being with your fear is about having a way of thinking and talking about it without defence. That increases the energy of the power of the fear, not the fear itself.

(I know it sounds like 'the force is with you', but if you let go, it really is!)

It's a good day to die
NATIVE AMERICAN SAYING (not Klingon!)

I'm not dead yet
MONTY PYTHON, *Monty Python and the Holy Grail*

One particular tribe of Native Americans would go into battle as a way of expressing their power, with no intent to kill, just to show their power. They would gallop into battle armed with nothing but small sticks, and would ride up and tap their surprised enemies on the shoulder.

They call this Collecting Coups. They felt this was far more warrior-like behaviour than depending on weapons and the death of another to be successful.

The Native Americans, the Buddhist monks and the Samurai warriors have one thing in common: they did not fear disappointment or disappointing.

So if you have hung in there over the last few pages, you may be wondering (I did say may be), how this relates to everyday life. Well, I guess I am using it as an extreme example of how if you take away the ultimate fear, the fear of death, you seem to be ready to take more risks, have a lower expectation and no fear of disappointment. I think it is a way of getting you to think of a bigger picture than just why you fear disappointing or letting your parents down.

So, let us go back there – to other people.

In fearing disappointment or disappointing, we don't only choose people to be dependent on. Disappointing and/or frustrating events can lead to anxiety, obsessive thoughts or dependencies which we cannot leave alone. Addictions can be to lifestyles, drugs, people, work, religion. Addiction is any dependency that self-perpetuates or self-catalyses at an ever-accelerating rate. What is the difference between "I'll just have one more drink" and "I'll practice that piano piece one more time"?

Addiction and obsession are about doing things in order to avoid something unpleasant; something we fear may happen if we don't have the drink or arrange the cutlery in the right way. Habits become addictive if enough is never enough; if perfect is not correct; if the reward and the work are inversely proportioned.

Do you often feel as though the sands are shifting beneath your feet?
Do you often worry that things will work out all right?
Do you often experience breathlessness and confusion?

This is a fear of disappointment which gets played out by you being anxious.

There was a psychological experiment done many years ago on a dog which illustrates this anxiety. The dog was taught that on hearing a high-pitched tone, it had to press a lever in order to avoid getting a mild shock. A low-pitched tone meant the opposite, that it must avoid pressing the lever in order to avoid a shock. The scientists gradually began to raise the low pitch and lower the high pitch until it became less and less clear which one was which. The dog became extremely anxious, starting to press the lever, then recoiling in a spasm of uncertainty.

One thing that might help you explore some of your fears is to ask yourself
questions about anxiety:

> What are the shocks you are trying to avoid?
>
> What are the levers that you press?
>
> What situations get you confused?

Safe is not the same as habitual. How many of your rituals are about personal
safety, and not familiarity?

Someone who is prone to anxiety is still trying coping responses. However their
belief is that there are perpetual terrors everywhere, and that the only hope
may be the extreme and constant use of coping responses – in this extreme
version, sometimes obsessive rituals such as excessive cleanliness or tidiness.
Extremely stressful.

It isn't in the clear-cut realms that we experience anxiety. It is in the grey,
confusing areas. Like life.

The world is full of possible peril and, like the dog, we scramble to work out
the rules for being safe.

Addictions and obsessions are similar to what computer programmers refer to as a 'do-loop'. A 'do-loop' is when an activity or routine keeps on going and repeating itself long after its usefulness is over. It keeps on 'doing'. The nature of ecosystems, humans and animals involves a level of routine. All the routines involve end conditions or exits. We keep doing the task until the end conditions are met. Normally, then, we stop. Sound right to you?

However, it is possible for these end conditions to be omitted, or missed so that the routine is carried out indefinitely, compulsively, until disorders and breakdowns occur and the whole system crashes (nervous breakdown, drinking binge, walking out of work). On the interminable and impossible search for perfection, when we get caught in obsessive behaviour, we are stuck in a 'do-loop', with no instantly visible exit. (Think hamster and wheel.)

So, you have met perfection; now meet its ugly sister, procrastination. They are both heading for the same car wreck.

Procrastination is a form of 'don't-loop', from which you can exit at any time. When the fear of perfect is so strong that it keeps us inert, we don't do anything. This is a cycle of repression and blockage, like a muscle spasm or depression. When we are on this cycle, the exit condition fires off continuously, never allowing us to maintain the activity, always finding an excuse to stop. In this state, we find any excuse not to do something, from rational objections to complete withdrawal.

"OK, I get it, but how do I unstick myself from this cycle?" you say.

The only way to unstick yourself from the cycle is to find what is creating the crossed signal and switch it back; that is, to recognise and accept the fear for what it is, without creating behaviours to mask it, defend against it, or hide it.

Sorry. I didn't say it would be easy.

How do you do it, difficult though it may be?

Keep asking yourself questions.
Challenge your assumptions about what and why you do things.
Don't be frightened if you answer "I don't know".
Being aware and asking the questions is a start. If you don't believe you have questions to ask than you are very, very stuck.

Searching for what has disappointed you in the past is hard. Owning that people disappoint you in the present is hard.

So our responses to fear disappointment could be any of the following:

Obsessiveness	*compulsively sticking to one thing*
Procrastination	*compulsively avoiding one thing*
Addiction /fidgeting	*avidly attaching to each passing thing*
Anger	*resentment and defence against*
	anything, particularly a change
Anxiety	*fear of everything around you*
Withdrawal/withholding	*shutting away anything and from anything*

Discovering what your behaviours are under pressure is hard to find out because the very thing you are seeking to find is also your means of searching for it. The distortion in the way we think distorts your efforts to correct the distortion. Trying harder increases the pressure.

Trying harder can't make you spontaneous; it's like trying to slam a revolving door!
KEITH JOHNSTONE

STOP TRYING, particularly if you are not sure what you are trying to do.

I can almost hear you say "but if I don't try, I won't get anywhere". I don't mean stop attempting, I mean stop pushing and contorting yourself to find *the* answer. Accepting that it's important is probably more important than the answer. The answer for me comes in the 'perfect' solution category. Obsessive and delusional.

Can you remember times in your life when you really didn't *try* and just let yourself do it? We usually go into heavy 'try' mode when we don't trust ourselves. When you watch any sportsman, artist or expert 'trying', you usually think there is something wrong. Many will tell you that their best work has been done when they were distracted by things physical or mental. Being, as opposed to doing, allows automatic processes to take over, and there are many parts of our brain that are actually more talented than our socially-adjusted selves. Our view of the world may be governed by the way others see us, but our need to please others is going to get in the way of knowing what *we* want. Living with our fear, with all its random variables, is part of the way we learn to free ourselves to be who we are, not what we think others want us to be.

Owning your fear of disappointment or disappointing means knowing what is important to you, not to anyone else.

So if you are still looking for the answer, in terms of you wanting the solution *now*, what is that about? Are you someone the words "Shut up, sit down and wait!" drive to distraction? What is the fear for you in waiting?

For me, I always felt that there was something I might be missing; I always get things very quickly, and once I have, I want to do whatever it is that is necessary. I think my fear was that I might miss an opportunity for an experience; but when I ask myself "so what if you do?" part of it is so that I can learn something and gain something intrinsically for myself. That need for challenge is largely about my own personal growth and learning. Why is that so important? I am not sure. I enjoy the buzz, and the proving to myself that I can do something. Does that mean I am scared that I can't? Does it mean that I need someone else to notice me doing all those things, and consequently say how wonderful I am? I don't think so. I don't think so because I very rarely tell people what I do. In fact, I find it embarrassing. My fear is that they would think I was boastful, boring and self-absorbed. My fear is being a burden or a bore.

(So why are you writing books, you ask? That's easy. It then becomes your choice whether you pick it up or decide it's not worth the trees. The challenge is can I do another one? I think I have come to enjoy the presence of that fear, the *can I do it?* one. The one about being a burden to others is not enjoyable, but less of a struggle.)

Enough self disclosure (see the burden fear again). I was using it to illustrate the point that even when you know about all this stuff, you still have to accept it and get on with it and that's the constant journey.

After two near-death experiences in as many years, I think I have become even more phlegmatic than I used to be; I still want to do things *now* – maybe even more than I used to. However, I don't feel desperate to do that any more. My fear that I might not do everything I wanted to before I die, or that I might miss out on the one great thing has gone from foreground to background. It matters less.

Joe was a musician experiencing 'writers block'. He was totally incredulous at the amount of time he had spent worrying about not writing. When asked what all the obsessing and defending was about, he replied that he thought it was to do with actually putting pen to paper. For him the most frightening thing about that was a disappointment in the experience. Rather than writing something which might disappoint or be disappointing, Joe kept himself away from imagined disappointment. He had idealised his own, and perceived need of others for everything he wrote to be perfect. He needed to learn to be able to write, not write the perfect song. Taking risks freed him up to be more creative, not less.

The mistaken belief that if you isolate yourself, then nothing bad happens becomes relatively safe but unrewarding and potentially obsessional. We get depressed when confronted with impermanance, or we devalue what we see and push it away.

If you continue to believe that you have control over fears or circumstances that are beyond your control, you may end up treating it as your fault when the inevitable happens. In this perverse way, of course, you will never disappoint yourself or others, because it will always be your fault. I would probably describe that as victim status and in some cases martyrdom. Nice and safe, and nobody would ever have high expectations, so you could never fail or disappoint. Good plan.

If that feels satisfying, then you have no reason to stop. Read no further, you will only get anxious about the number of options that may be open to you. In fact, why on earth would you want to read something like this if you were satisfied? Please don't say "curiosity" – my bullshit meter will sound major alarm bells. Who are you trying to fool?

You are either satisfied or you are not.

Feeling uncomfortable or just irritated?

Don't be disappointed in yourself or me. Ask yourself what you are feeling and what is causing you to feel it.

Interestingly, people who take on this kind of position are frequently the same people who rescue others:

> "Don't worry about it, it's not your fault."
>
> "It's not something anyone could have done anything about."
>
> "You tried your best, the economy is lousy anyway."
>
> "The best manager in the world would not have been able to manage him."

This is all about minimising another's perception of control while raising your own in a rather subtle way: "I can comfort you – depend on me."

When society is at its most callous, it shifts the blame and attributes greater levels of control than could have actually existed:

> "She was asking for it." (Rape victims have the power to prevent the rape.)
>
> "If only they had made the effort to assimilate, they wouldn't have these problems." (Minorities have the power to prevent their persecution.)

OK, time to pause and drink wine... tea... coffee...

Glass half empty or half full?

Andrew's fear of disappointing and disappointment was so strong that he had to not only assess the people around him and punish them for their ability to disappoint, but had also to do the same for himself. It was like a continuum on which he observed something someone did and then assessed it. For example, Tom, his colleague, is a lightweight. He would then go on in his head to say "lightweight – bad". That progressed to bad, doesn't deserve good, must be punished. The punishment, in this case, usually took the form of some kind of withholding of expertise so that Tom looked stupid in front of others.

When it was described to Andrew in this way, he said "But that's stupid. I wasn't thinking about it like that."

"And now that it has been described to you in that way, do you see yourself doing it?"

Knowing smile of the found out from Andrew.

He had been described by his boss as always seeing things as half empty, not half full. His boss had been unable to articulate any more clearly what he meant, but when Andrew looked at his interactions honestly, he could see that there was a pattern. It was to only see people as bad. This meant that all his solutions to situations were about defending himself against the bad. The glass was half empty. Here it comes, the 'so what do I do' question. "So how do I change that?" "Well, it's more of a coming to terms with the fact that you do it. Without an acceptance of that, there is nothing for you to change. It is not about what you do, but how you see others."

This is the point where most people get puzzled and confused. Changing one's mental model of how we see others often involves a reversal of thinking. In Andrew's case, when asked to describe how he would deal with the glass half full, he struggled to find any solutions that might suggest that kind of mental model. He soon became very aware of how narrow his thinking was, and how difficult it was for him to imagine a different worldview.

To see a world where the glass was half full.

His seeing himself in action was a crucial turning point in his 'what do
I do now' process. He had to see himself thinking in that way, and appreciate
its possible outcome before he could begin to think differently.

To assess people as lightweight was fine in itself; it was what he did
next with the assessment that damaged his ability to influence others. He
needed to learn to assess and accept and stop there; not move to judging and
punishing. If he could learn to accept, there would be no need to punish. To do
this he had to learn to be with his fear of disappointment.

He saw the keys right in front of him, but took them himself and hid
them in his own pocket. He knew where they were all the time.

He had created his own shadows.

We cling to what we have or remove ourselves from it, so that we don't
experience either our own or others' vulnerabilities. By doing this, we miss the
opportunities that we seek to connect and experience. It is not about having no
attachment but about becoming less controlling and proscriptive about how that
might happen. Being with your fears is about neither clinging nor rejecting. By
stopping these activities it changes the way we experience situations and
ourselves.

*Are you able to see
yourself differently?*

Fear of disappointing always ends up in disappointment.

The fear of finding the keys becomes more powerful than the joy or practicality of finding them.

fear of disappointment

"There is something to be learned from a rainstorm. When meeting with a sudden shower you try to get wet and run quickly along the road. By doing such things as passing under the eaves of a house you still get wet. When you are resolved from the beginning, you will not be perplexed, though you will still get the same soaking. This understanding extends to all things."

– GHOST DOG *(THE WAY OF THE SAMURAI)*

Our deepest fear is not that we are
inadequate.
Our deepest fear is that we are
Powerful beyond measure.
It is our light, not our darkness,
That frightens us.
MARIANNE WILLIAMSON

fear of success

Fear of being found out.
Fear of not being found out.
Fear of failure.
Fear of success.

Frightened of success; why would anyone be frightened of succeeding? In a way, if you succeed the you have much further to fall.

Tim, despite his desire to be liked (or because of it), has enormous difficulty in accepting positive feedback. He wants to be successful, but seems to have a fear of anyone voicing it. It seems to be OK for other people to think it, but not to say it out loud. Part of him will enjoy the attention, and another part will squirm at being thought of as boastful or complacent. Yet another, more complex, part of him will not want to believe it for fear that it might not be true, and that he has fooled everyone and is about to get found out. "Sooner or later someone is going to find me out. I can't continue to be successful. Someone is going to open the box marked 'me' and see that there really is nothing there."

This is by no means an uncommon feeling; hands up how many of you find this description familiar? It is particularly common among high achievers, not surprisingly. No matter how advanced we become we fear that people will find us out to be fakes. I often find myself in a room full of successful people, all of whom are afraid to speak up for fear of looking stupid, being the only one who doesn't get it. Only when we are all comfortable with the fact that we are not the only one who feels that way, will we admit to what we fear, and hence can begin learning.

Is this a fear of success, or a fear of what it might mean to be successful?

Sometimes we feel so overwhelmed by the expectation of success; if people come to expect wonders, and we don't always deliver, then we become damned forever as failures.

The playwright John Osborne writes about his characters' fear of failing. His characters all present as angry, probably because the chances of realizing our 'dreams' are few, and we are so locked into this that when the chances do appear, we are likely to miss them. His characters have no idea how to put the nightmare away, how to forget it, repress it or even talk about it. They live in permanent fear; half-truths experienced as whole truths. We are all capable of making half-truths whole truths. We can all identify a little with the pressures that lead to a Billy Liar. Osborne call this the "comfortless tragedy of isolated hearts". Their fear of failure and success is entangled with a fear and reality about being alone, as opposed to being on their own.

Ships are safest in the harbour, but that isn't what they were built for.

So a fear of failure becomes a fear of success.

Whenever I work with people on 360° feedback, they are always much keener to talk about their low scores than their high ones. The usual reasons given for this include:

"The high scores are ok, it's what I need to work on that's important...'
"They would say that; they're too scared to tell the truth...'
When faced with the logic that if these comments were true, than they would only have either high scores or low scores, not a mixture of the two, most people either squirm uncomfortably in their chair, or uncontrollably smirk the smirk of being caught.

Failing is not failure. You can not succeed at something, but that does not mean that you are a failure as a person.

John had been struggling with risk taking in his work for some time. He was highly regarded by his bosses, his peers and his team, and was promoted for being an effective manager (unusual in itself, the cynics among you might say). However, when he got promoted to senior management, he discovered that it wasn't enough for him just to do his job effectively. He was expected to think strategically and therefore make more long-term and possibly risky decisions. This scared him, and so he just kept his head down and carried on with the operational side of his job. This meant that he ended up missing out on some crucial business opportunities because he wasn't looking. He said that he found it impossible to make long-term decisions in case he got it wrong. Day-to-day decisions he felt he could put right. When I asked what he thought would happen if he got it wrong, he said he would have failed. I asked him what he would have failed at, and he said his job. I then asked him "Why do you think that getting it wrong means you have failed in your job?"

"Because I didn't get it right."

"Why do you think that is a failure?"

"Because it is."

"By whose standards is it a failure?"

"OK, OK, I get it..." You can probably guess the rest of the conversation. John had been convinced that if you did one thing wrong, then you were a failure. There was no grey area in between; one brick out, the house falls down. Do not pass Go, do not collect £200. Failure. It was not the view of anyone he worked for.

Just his own fear of failure. However that is often the judgement we feel others make of us; and indeed in our intolerance, that we make of others. If you do it wrong you are stupid.

We fear being judged and in doing so, we judge others rather than tolerate or accept. Our fear of being judged extends to both success and failure. We can be as bad at accepting positive feedback as negative criticism. We use it to put others in a negative position so that we can feel better about ourselves. Why would you do that?

Fran had a reputation for not suffering fools gladly. She was incredibly intolerant, and didn't care who knew it. (At least that's what she said.) People in one way admired her directness, and in another were frightened of her very poisonous barbs. This began to be an issue for her as she had to operate more in the political environment at work; to the point where, after a succession planning interview, she was told that unless she was able to be less 'vicious' with others, she would not reach the next level of management.

This was a huge shock to her as she had got this far on her ability to get things done, which she attributed directly to her direct, no-nonsense style. In part, it was. But it was limited.

When she was questioned about why she felt the need to be so blunt, she said people were idiots and not really worth the space they occupied. She said she had no time for fools. A fool was someone who, in Fran's book, did not think as she did, could not 'get it' fast enough for her, and who was not responsive enough in their actions.

Fran had done something many of us do. She had a scale on which she subconsciously rated people.

Like Fran, fab and worthy ——————————— **complete idiots**

This is a JUDGEMENT scale. An idiot meter. (Actually, Fran called it her 'tosser meter'.)

As soon as someone appears on this scale, it is impossible for you to respond to or influence them. You have judged them as unworthy and treat them as such. What did this mean for Fran?

So the flow of Fran's behaviour went from:

They don't get it ———— **they're stupid** ———— **dismiss them**
(that's dismiss as in be dismissive about them, not fire them....)

What Fran had to learn was how to see other people as not getting it, or not being as quick as she was, and stop there. Before she judged and dismissed them. So they didn't get it, or they disagreed; so they were maybe even thick. Did she need to punish them for being stupid by dismissing them? This was a big realisation for her; that she was punishing them. Accepting them had not occurred to her. Were they really stupid? What could she do to contribute to better communication with them?

This not only had an effect at work, it made Fran far more aware of her very dismissive attitude to her husband.

In being less judgemental and dismissive of others, Fran learned to be less judgmental and dismissive of herself.

She began to stop fearing her own success.

This may be something you relate to in many different ways; you may have many scales on which you judge people. It is worth taking a moment to reflect and maybe draw out a few scales and put the people you have the most difficulty with on them.

Try it!

So, given that this fear of success manifests itself in many ways, how would you describe yourself?

    Do you claim to not be depressed or anxious?

    Would you describe yourself as happy, successful and accomplished?

    Do you like surprises and ambiguity?

If you answered yes to all of these questions, then you need only read the next bit out of smugness or curiosity.

We often speak about people who believe this with a hint of envy saying "I wish I had your discipline; everything seems to come so easily to you; how do you do it?"

The answer, as ever, is not that simple. When you examine the way these people live their lives you discover a different kind of defence mechanism. They aren't depressed or anxious. They have a huge need for social conformity, a discomfort with ambiguity, and a fear of risk.

How would you recognise one (or yourself)?

They usually feel a strong need to plan things. They may even be able to tell you what they will be having for dinner in two weeks' time. Behaviours are either right or wrong, people are either good or bad, the world is black or white. They tend to speak in absolute terms; no shades of grey. They use words like never and always. They keep a very tight lid on their emotions and are seen as stoic, hard-working, solid people who never stand out in a crowd. They lack emotional expression; no talking about messy feelings, and little recognition of those messy things in others. Their feelings are usually expressed in very clear-cut terms with little tolerance for subtle blends or secondary emotions.

So are they terribly fearful but not even aware of it? Some are; look back, for example, at John (page 000). Some who repress their feelings will give away more if they are assured that their responses will be confidential and won't invite disapproval. And there are some who seem OK; mentally healthy, productive and socially interactive. But they often have high physiological stress responses. They work very hard to generate a world without ambiguity or surprises. That takes a lot of strain and effort, particularly as the world is full of surprises and ambiguity. Small wonder their minds may not react with anxiety, but their bodies do. It is incredibly stressful to try to create a world without stress, without fears. Sooner or later, the fears enter the security compound by some means or other.

So who are you?

What impact does your fear of failure have on your ability to deal with ambiguity?
How are you with grey?

"I don't want any trouble."
"Life is trouble; only death isn't."
ZORBA THE GREEK

So how do we get caught in the black and white of success and failure? Parents encourage their children to excel, but only along accepted lines and woe betide them if they celebrate that success. So children may end up haunted by the fear that even if they express themselves successfully they may not be accepted.

So if your biggest fear is discovery that you are nothing, that's it. It *is* a void. And?

Amy told me about how frightened she is that, despite her tangible track record in building the successful administration system of a large school, when it came down to it she had actually achieved very little. Despite her results and her success, she is terrified they will find her out... find out what? She feels a level of emptiness but how little right she feels she has to feel good about what she does. The school don't tell her they appreciate her enough for her; but could they ever tell her so much that she would feel good? I doubt it.

She is terrified that despite all the work she has done, the concrete proof of her achievements and abilities, that she will be found as having nothing. She has a bottomless pit of recognition which no one could fill. So what is it she won't let them give her?

What on earth could they say that would change her mental model?

She has to believe that she is somewhere different as opposed to making a list of actions she has to do.

She has set herself up to fail no matter what people do. Only she can change that.

What would you want to say to her?

The fear of being nothing. A void.

Touching the void. Let's go there for a while. Touching the void.

Our instinctive response to fear is to contract against it. In childbirth, the only drug-free way to even vaguely bear the pain of contractions is to learn to breathe and go with it. The same is true of defending against fear. It doesn't ease the fear, it increases it. When you can't hold on any more, there is an opening that can't happen when you are trying to control yourself. It's that opening that allows you to begin to touch the fear. Back to the void: the feeling of being nothing inside is often worse than empty, it feels as though what we have inside is all rubbish. It feels like one massive delusion, full of undigested hopes and expectations. When you actually own this mess, it all starts to dissipate and the void appears.

The void is us at our most powerful when we go there. When we think about it, it is one of the scariest places on earth but, when you actually yield and go there, it is where we are best equipped to deal with the slings and arrows of our lives.

This is the point where we need to stop taking photos and just have the experience.
Experience the shadows.

Stop and feel this bit... it's heavy.

Why should I? you say.

What would I get if I did?

You might get:

an answer to whatever it is you are struggling with;

a sense of what really matters and what can be let go;

a strong belief that you will be OK.

Good reasons to go there...

Many stories are told of scientists who, when desperately stuck on a problem, find that their long sought for leap comes to them when they are shopping or dreaming. One Scottish physicist is alleged to have said "The bus, the bath and the bed. That's where the great discoveries are made in our science."

Not doing can often be more productive than doing. The void.

Many people who have a near-death experience have a flash of really strong emotion about what is really important for them, because all defences have been stripped away, and the only thing that remains in that moment of clarity is you and who and what is important to you. In that moment you really touch your void, you touch that part that is inexplicable, non-repeatable, sometimes indescribable. Because that is frequently its nature, it constitutes neither failure nor success, but a void.

Different people feel the void in their own ways. For Joe Simpson, the mountaineer and climber, it was a depth to himself that was beyond anything he could have imagined or dreamt. Some people, having touched that place, do not want to be far from it: hospice workers sit in the presence of death; many people enjoy past lives.

It may well be that fear of loss stops people from touching the void. If you are attached to things and people, you fear loss of them. Those who have most to lose are usually the most defended.

The people of the most defended nation on earth are the most attached to what they have and the most fearful of what they might lose. This is the nation that put success above everything. The city that was most traumatized by suicide bombers is a city built on success, where its major monuments are not to church or state but to commerce and success. In a way, fear of loss is fear of attachment. Fear of failure is fear of success. Suicide bombers, on the other hand, have nothing to lose, and are not attached to anything material. They have no fear of failure. Neither do Buddhist monks. The Buddhist aim is to be relieved of a need for attachments, so that they have little to fear. When you have a religion that embraces death before, during and after, and souls who want to be relieved of attachments, then you have people who are free to be.

So the fear of loss or failure ends up being the most likely cause of failure.
How's that for irony?
Fear of ruin can destroy.

Sometimes that strong attachment – a.k.a. fear of loss – feels so scary, that
instead of going with it, you become convinced that if you focus hard enough
on it, that you can make it *not* happen. Sort of King Canute syndrome. You *will*
make those waves go back.

Sound delusional?
Have you ever heard yourself or others say things like this?
"Once I make up my mind to do something, I stay with it until the job is
done."
"When things don't go the way I want them, it just makes me work even
harder."
"It's so hard to train new people. It's so much quicker to do it myself, and I get
the job done properly."

The illusion of control.

If you have uttered these immortal phrases, then you probably believe that, with enough determination and effort, you can conquer everything and anything. In a world that is constantly changing, this leaves no room for error or adaptation. It also implies a sense of omnipotence and an drive for perfection.

Sherman James described this illusion of control as John Henryism. This refers to an American hero who tried to outpace a steam drill tunneling through a mountain by hammering a six foot long steel drill. He did beat the machine, and then fell dead from the effort. The everyday manifestation of this belief is irritability, dissatisfaction and frustration. The physical manifestations are tiredness, hypertension and stress-related diseases. Even individuals who know this intellectually find it hard to let go of the need emotionally.

The model for this is usually deeply rooted in messages that say 'be perfect', 'nine out of ten isn't good enough' or 'how did everyone else do?'

One individual – Rosa – whom I was discussing this with grinned broadly and heaved a sigh of relief. "I now know why I have been driving myself and my family mad for the last twenty years. My family had very strong ideas about how children should behave and what was acceptable behaviour. Not being the perfect child was not an option. It has meant that I have sometimes, without knowing, pushed these ideals onto the people around me, both at work and at home; because I am also seeing perfect as the only option. Now how do I stop it, and what would I do instead?"

It is that last question that haunts most people who have a fear of not being good enough.

That if they stop doing what they have always done, if they stop being perfect, they will be found out as lacking and not good enough.

The illusion of this fear is as great as the illusion of perfection.

For Rosa, it was a very real feeling that she experienced as a child, and was probably founded in her experience of punishment when she was not 'perfect'. However, that does not mean she has to continue to both respond in the same way, and push others to respond in the same way. The feelings and fears she experienced as a child were real, but they need to be separated from her current reality. She is a more diverse person, with more experience than the child she once was, and the people around her have different drives.

Ambition is the last refuge of the failure.
OSCAR WILDE

So what is it with so called 'high achievers'? They always need to be doing, and can't just be. What would you be seeing if you met one of these high achiever, 'doing' persons?

> Do you find yourself being impatient and curt with others?
> Do you find yourself envious of the way others live their lives?
> Do little things really irritate you?

If you answered yes to all of these questions, (or know someone who would), you may well have a propensity to being a 'Type A' personality. Type A personalities are immensely competitive, overachieving, time-pressured, impatient and hostile. These people are deeply unappreciative of others; their fear being that they need all the approval and recognition themselves, so they cannot give any away for fear there won't be any left for them.

Out of all these characteristics, hostility has emerged as the only significant predictor of heart disease. Some people suggest that at the heart of the hostility is a time pressure: "I can't waste my time here; it's quicker to do it myself", and that the core of the time pressure is insecurity. I would take that one step further, and suggest that it's a fear of failing and/or being found out to be a fraud that is behind the hostile behaviour. There is no time to savour anything you have achieved, you are always on to the next thing. There is no way you could possibly enjoy anything anyone else has done as that might belittle you in some way; also you have to rush off and prove yourself again – or at least hide from the world for another day that you are really a fraud.

People who are hostile perceive other people as deliberately getting in the way of their success. People with high levels of dissatisfaction with their lives often express this in terms of blame for others; blaming the government, their tools, their parents without actually expressing anger. Type A people believe that life is full of menacing fears and stressors that demand responses of a particularly hostile nature. The smallest irritation can provoke a disproportionate reaction. They are always on edge, and one of the stories that is told about the discovery of Type A comes from the cardiologists, Friedman and Rosenman, who researched and documented the type. They were spending a lot of money having to re-upholster their chairs. When a new upholsterer came in to check out the problem he asked what was wrong with the patients, as all of the chairs were damaged in the same way. He remarked that people did not normally wear out seats in this fashion. Only the front few inches of the seat cushion and of the padded armrests were torn to shreds. The patients in the waiting rooms all habitually sat on the edge of their seats, fidgeting and scratching at the arm rests.

Those who have a fear of failure do; they frequently sit on the edge of their seats, literally and metaphorically, for fear that they might miss something or do it wrong. It is this very fear which stops them being in the moment and seeing opportunities. The fear stops them being able to respond, they are too involved in the emotions of fear. So their fear comes true, they miss the opportunity and fail.

Ready, aim; Ready, aim; Ready, aim... unable to fire.

Not ready to fire. Would rather not fire than miss. If I prepare enough I will get it right the first time, but they never fire...

Sitting on the edge of your chair also means you give yourself no support.

Do you sit forward in your chair?

What would it be like for you to sit back in your chair, making use of your whole body?
Try it.

R: So I am still nervous that if I stop what I am doing and stop
        being ambitious, that I will fail.

Q: *What leads you to believe that?*

R: Well, that others will catch me up.

Q: *And then what will happen?*

R: I won't be in the lead anymore.

Q: *And how does being in the lead tell you that you are successful?*

R: Because I am doing it first... Ok, I don't know why doing it
        first would make me feel successful, but it does.

Q: *Who do you need to show?*

For them, fear of doing nothing means fear of failure; there will be nothing to
be recognized for.

Imagine a child throwing a tennis ball at a wall in the garden. Picture them
doing it again and again, looking absorbed and happy. When you picture this,
what do you feel?

As a parent you might feel a hope that this will increase their ball control, and
put them in line to be a Wimbledon champion.

You might feel frustrated that there has to be more productive things this child could do with their time then a seemingly boring, repetitive action with no perceived achievement.

You might think that they should be counting the number of times they catch the ball. (See how that thought crept in, despite the fact I told you to consider your *feelings...?*)

So why is this kid bouncing the ball off the wall? Maybe they are fascinated by the different directions and speeds and arcs they can create after the bounce, depending on their initial spin.

Perhaps they have no idea why they are doing it. Perhaps they just love being inside the rhythm of it.

Maybe it's not even activities like bouncing a ball; it could be listening to music, staring out of the window, singing in the shower.

For many of us the idea of being a 'couch potato' or doing nothing has become an even more difficult thing to do in current times. We have more means of communication than ever. Yesterday I watched a man talking on his mobile phone as he swam in the pool. A new fear of being seen to be unavailable, a fear of missing out, has not crept in, but *burst* in.

This is about taking being in the moment to obsessive extremes. By doing that of course you lose the opportunity to actually be in the moment.

I think it is about the confusion between what Fritz Perls called Respondable and Responsible. Respondable describes things you want to respond to, and Responsible describes things you feel responsible for. The need to be successful and not fail is tied up with duties and obligations. Being in the moment usually feels like it conflicts with that, making it hard to see how you could remain successful and BE.

What would you like to respond to in your job? This question is more about the person than the duty... it may be hard work, but it isn't necessarily about obligation. You can describe your responsibilities, your 'to do' lists.

Trappings and technology can have the effect of increasing responsibilities as opposed to respondency, which is how they are always sold to us. An automatic washing machine didn't help women, it just made it possible for them do something else while the clothes were being washed. It added to their responsibilities and duties. Email and mobile phones have the technology to increase our respondency, but because of our success drive, our fear of failure, they have come to increase responsibilities not abilities or capacities. How many of you choose to answer your phones? How many of you say you don't have a choice? What do you fear will happen if you don't answer?

The sense of 'busyness' and 'hurry up' that seems to pervade our society is providing a feeding frenzy for a fear of failure. As the pace hots up, the reaction to the fear increases the pace and the tension.

I listen to people who say they 'just' went and saw a film at the weekend, or 'just' played with their kids. Why have those means of being become something to be justified, as in 'just'. This says 'mea culpa, I have sinned and not produced a tangible result of my activities. This was all I did.' Why do we feel the need to say that? Why are we so defensive about just being? It's obviously quite difficult to do for most people, because few people do it unconditionally. This need for achievement, this fear of 'no results, no success, equals failure' is a huge factor in the raised stress levels of most people today. We even call people who appear to do nothing, who just go with the flow, 'slackers'.

Have we become 'just doing cultures?'

Even people's leisure activities seem geared to achievement. You can't enjoy a day on a hill, you have to climb Everest; you don't cook for pleasure, you 'entertain' your friends and perform; you don't have time to smell the roses because everything else needs repotting or tending to...

Is the opposite to a high achiever a lazy bastard? That certainly seems to be one of the fears; that you will be considered lazy.

In not appreciating or even valuing the activities which have no measurable result, or even a point, we could be turning away from the most precious things about the activity:

■ that they are what we WANT to do, not feel a need or obligation to do.

■ they are something we feel passionately about.

Passion can be very disdainful of reason and productivity. It can also be very fragile, particularly when confronted by our embarrassment and impatience. But it does hold the promise for growth and new life and it is at the heart of desire.

How many allegedly 'useless' activities do you indulge in? If fear rules your life, it isn't enough.

Find some and enjoy them.

Float, don't swim.

We teach people how to remember, we never teach them how to grow.
OSCAR WILDE

What a crucial comment. We spend most of our school life learning to regurgitate what the exam system expects of us – for FEAR we would fail or not please the system. Who told the system what to expect of us? How does it know it is the right thing for us or the system? The spirit of the importance of remembering as opposed to being or learning stays with us through our working life. We see situations that we remember, not experience and learn from.

We have the experience and miss the meaning.

It's like taking photographs on holiday instead of experiencing it. I remember being in Angkor Wat in Cambodia; for me one of the most extraordinary places on the planet. I had gone there to watch the sun rise. There I was, at 5 o'clock in the morning, with a large number of Japanese tourists waiting with our cameras ready to snap the sun coming over the temple.

It didn't oblige. It was gloomy and cloudy. So we took pictures anyway, and most of the Japanese wandered back to their hotels to get breakfast. I decided to take advantage of the early hour and the lack of people to go and get some photographs of the spookier parts of the temple. Why did I want the photographs? Did I want to prove something to myself and others about where I had been? How clever my photographs were? Did I not trust my memory? All of the above?

Well, my camera's battery went dead. Horror of horrors, I was faced with just being in a place, not photographing it. Being with it, not externalizing it as something to be 'taken'. Was my need for control really that big?

Why was I frightened of not taking photographs?

Whatever the answers to all those questions, I did stay with it. I let go and sat watching and experiencing sounds and sights as the light crept over the temple. What an experience. I have nothing to prove I was there, nothing to show. What I have is mine and in my head and heart. It's hard to even explain in words, but it doesn't matter. I can smile as I think of that feeling.

The next time you zip into action to snap a sunrise or a view, don't.
Just be there.
Don't do, be.

It's Sinatra's world...
we just live in it!

Just as an afterthought, if you're not *doing* anything, then you have no criteria for success. You do not succeed or fail if you are being. Maybe the pedants among you would say that there must be criteria for being. I think the only criterion is that if you're not being, you are doing.

Don't have the experience and miss the meaning.

Is that too much doing and being for you?
Let's just recap.
This may seem removed from a fear of success. I don't believe it is. I believe we get hooked into producing external, tangible results of what we do, as opposed to internal knowledge and experience. We are only unskilled at describing these internal feelings and experiences because we don't have the practice. The more we do it, the more we are able to understand and describe what it means for ourselves. But first you have to let go and have the experience *without* the hindrance of a success or failure criterion.

You have to be prepared to not find the keys in order to have the courage to go looking for them.
Are you frightened of picking up the keys?

fear *of success*

I had to arrive at the brink and then take a leap into the dark.

HENRY MILLER

The human spirit may crave freedom
but it recoils from choice...
ANDREW ANTHONY

fear of choice

Fear of freedom.

There is an apocryphal tale of James Joyce asking Carl Jung what the difference was between his own mind and that of his schizophrenic daughter. "She falls," Jung is said to have replied. "You jump!"
Freedom to choose......

Do we or don't we have a choice?
Marx (Karl, not Groucho) suggested that men make their own destinies, but not necessarily in circumstances of their own choosing. How we interpret and make sense of the events that happen is the key to our ability and desire to choose. I believe that the choice is there more often than we care to admit it.

What prevents us choosing is our fear of freedom.
Fear of being accountable.

Whenever we feel that we might be wrong, we won't make a choice.
Whenever we feel we run the risk of being blamed we won't make a choice.

We fear how other people will judge us; so you could argue that fear of choice is a fear of disapproval and/or disappointment, and I guess it is, but it is such an important part of being who you are, that it deserves special notice.

If you like, choosing is a manifestation of what it is like to know your fear and not feel paralysed by it. So you might be aware that you are frightened of your boss's disapproval, and yet still feel able to make a choice and do something risky, and feel comfortable with the consequences.

"I am so anxious to do what is right, that I forgot to do what is right."
JANE AUSTEN, *Mansfield Park*

What conditions would need to be present to get you to this position, rather than the more common no-risk option of doing nothing that wouldn't be approved of?

For me, there are big differences between a choice and a decision. Most of us, when faced with a problem, experience the dilemma of choice. A choice is more to do with an understanding of you in the situation. It is often a much more systemic thought process affecting more than one aspect of our lives. It frequently revolves around what issues are important, rather than actions that need to be taken.

Choice, by its nature, is about freedom, in that it is about what you *want*, not what you *should*.

So that demands that, first of all, you know what you want.

Most of us fall at that hurdle. We either don't want to answer the question, or think it will take too long or, more often, assume we know.
It is that basic assumption that needs to be questioned.
We often confuse expectations with desires and wants. What we expect may come from what we want; it may also come from what we fear. The fear may not just be of something 'bad', such as 'failure', it may also be of something that was nominally 'good', such as success.

If we have expectations, we have not necessarily made a choice; in fact it is very unlikely. The expectations may be what we think other people expect, or what we should expect.

See how complicated we can make life?

These expectations are often closely linked with a sense of nostalgia for a past that may or may not have happened. The 'happy' family, the 'dream' house, the 'romantic' partner. We often hope for a future that will be better without looking at what 'better' means.

In addition to the chance blows to which life subjects everyone else, we add the needless suffering that comes from impossible demands that we be special, and that the world be fair and just.
SHELDON KOPP

When you make a choice, you know what you want (not need).
You know what it will take.
You know what you will lose and what that will cost.

Most importantly of all you accept the implications of choosing.

That is, you accept that what you do will bring something, and whatever that something is, you will be comfortable with it. This is really tough. It means you are the only one responsible and accountable for what happens. (Including how you deal with any intervention by the slings and arrows of outrageous fortune.) So, six months down the line, if you have made a choice to do something, even if it didn't work out the way you had planned, you are still comfortable with the choice. People who have made a true choice, don't look back, they are free to be with whatever happens.

Neither either or – always both and.
JEAN HOUSTON

No wonder we rarely make choices; we often drift into things or say "I might as well" or "here goes". These are decisions, not choices.

So what is a decision then?

When you make a decision it is much more grounded in external criteria. A choice is based on internal criteria; what I want.

A decision is usually tied to duty, need, obligation and any other external criteria.

As such it is easy not take responsibility for it, because its rationale and logic are external to you. It is much more objectively based. As such it is hard to get passionate about it, or commit to it in its deepest sense.

The external issues are not things we make up, and are not necessarily defences. They are real. It is whether those issues are at the heart of what we do (decision) or whether they are additional to something we want (choice).

Decisions do not leave you free. Only a choice makes you free.

Freedom has the cost of accountability attached to it.

Decisions don't come with the internal power to enforce them.

Power comes with choice.

Freedom is accountability.

Are you ready, accepting and grounded enough to do that?

It's *mine.* I did it.

Anne doesn't know what she wants. She knows she can do her current job standing on her head and needs more. She has been offered a job in the US by her employer and is really excited about it, but the job itself isn't that much different from what she is currently doing, and the main attraction would be the novelty of living in San Francisco. (You might consider that a big enough attraction; it isn't for her.)

At this moment in time, she doesn't know what it is she seeks in a job, and so it is impossible for her to make a choice. She has told her company that she will take the job in San Francisco, but she feels very dissatisfied. It would not be a disaster for her to go there, but it would not be her choice. She is making a decision based on a need for security, a loyalty to her company, and the fact that nothing else has popped up.

All external to her.

One of the difficulties is that now she has made her decision, it will be difficult for her to stop the processes that are already in motion with her company, work permits and the like. So making a decision has put the perceived power of choice even further away. Is it really?

Could she at any moment change her mind?

Of course she could, but she would have to have a really strong reason, and she is not likely to be in the free state of mind to do that with all the external pressures lurking.

What would you say to Anne?

Let's recap..

CHOICE	DECISION
I want	I need to
I ought, should	I feel and think
I think I am happy, content	Restless, maybe I could have, if only
I have lost..	I still have to
I know what has happened	What if…
Don't need to keep looking back	Keep rehashing what has happened
Acceptance	Knowledge
Yes and	Yes but
Subject	Object

That last one is really about how you see yourself in the situation; as subject or object. When you see yourself as an object, as someone to be controlled and directed in order to be at their most effective, you are most likely to use verbs like must, ought, should. You treat yourself as someone who must 'fit in'. Your aim becomes to complete your task in a way that will be most appreciated by others. You have handed control for choice to anything or anyone external.

This is about external value. The fear of making a choice in this state comes from a fear of not pleasing someone else, or failing. In this state, you end up making decisions.

When you see yourself as subject, as someone who is at their most effective when they operate from themselves, you are most likely to use verbs like want, wish, feel. The desire for the now means there is no fear. You treat yourself as someone who is important in themselves. This is about inner value. In this state, you feel free to make a choice.

Neither of these states is 'right' or 'wrong'.

If we operate purely as subject, free and unfettered, we end up without thought for rationale or others.
If we operate purely as object, determined and controlled, we become driven and unrelated to our experiences.

Kierkegaard calls living in this dual state "the dizziness of freedom". That's enough to make you fearful. In extreme reactions to the fear, we try to avoid the anxiety by abandoning ourselves to irresponsible freedom or by the opposite way of obsessionally controlling every action.

Freedom lies in the capacity to experience both states, knowingly. Knowing when you are doing something creative that you free yourself up and let irrational urges come into play. On the other hand, when studying for an exam, it may help to put yourself into the well controlled, objective, externally directed mode.

Courageous living in this dual state is, I believe, the source of our creativity. Most of our literature, art, theatre and cinema is built around our actions in the face of our contexts. We are drawn to and are inspired by the choices of others. Yet we are frightened of making our own.

It's really, REALLY, **REALLY** hard to make a choice.

Think about your life.

Based on the criteria we have talked about for choices, you can probably count on one hand the number you have made in your life. School, university, job, relationship, children; all the big, so-called choices have probably been made for you or have been decisions. The real choices you have made will have left you feeling content, no matter what outcome they had. They are also likely to be points in your life where you really felt you had changed. The difference explains why we think we have made choices, but have in fact taken decisions, and then wonder why we are still wanting... Many say they accept what has happened; what they really mean is they know what has happened; they don't necessarily accept it.

Speculation is so much safer than finding out the truth.
So where is the hard truth about choice?

Chris Argyris suggests that the more data you have about your environment, the more choice you have.
Jim March suggests that it doesn't matter how much data you have: risk will always be a determining and unpredictable variable of any choice.

Two great minds with divergent choice. Both probably correct. Is this an example of being able to hold two seemingly opposing views at the same time as an expression of a free mind? Or are they really opposing? Does it matter that you can see wisdom in both?

Challenge and question what seem to be opposing views in your life. How far apart are they in reality, or is it fear that keeps them apart?

There is no universal hard truth. For you to be able to choose, you need to know what your truth is. That means knowing what your fear(s) are.

Never confuse wisdom with luck.
FREEING RULE OF ACQUISITION #44

Have you ever felt like this?
      "I'm really sorry that I did it that way."
      "It would have been better if I…"
      "What I really wanted was….."

Fear is probably the most elemental and primordial of all human drives. It has the force to make people die or do things for no other reason than that they cannot imagine doing otherwise. If you have convinced yourself of this, and it takes you in the equation to convince, not just circumstances, than you will not believe you can do anything different.

Think about it…

Need comes out of fear.
That's why you can't make a choice out of fear.
It's why you can't commit from a place of fear.
It's why you never feel satisfied from a place of fear.

Two key fears help us avoid making choices:

Fear of loss and fear of hostility

When we make a choice, part of the difficulty is accepting what you will lose by making the choice, and dealing with that loss. Without that acceptance, six months down the line will probably see you regretting what you did. It always seems to be the hardest thing for people to accept: "Why do we have to lose something?" asked Henry, a frustrated Chief Executive, who was struggling to understand why change was not happening in his organisation. "Why can't we just choose to be something else and continue with everything else?"

A threat of loss creates anxiety, and actual loss, sorrow; both, moreover, are likely to arouse anger.
JOHN BOWLBY

Frequently it is the fear of loss that keeps us in the same position. When you actually examine what it would mean to lose something, it is smaller than we have held it to be. Maybe we won't know how important it is to us until we don't have it. Many people talk about how important their family becomes when one of them is ill. Or they only allow themselves to think of all the things they have ever wanted to do because they are sick, or come into a great deal of money. There is a reality here, clearly about what we need to survive in the world, and what we have to give up in order to do so. However, how much of that is what we want to have, rather than what we think we should or ought to have?

When something changes, you can never go back to exactly the way it was before, something will be different. If the word loss scares you, begin with what would be different, but progress to loss. It might be that you will never catch that train again, get good quality coffee, or be able to wear jeans to work. For some people those things would be more or less important.

Can you describe three things that you would never give up under any circumstances?

When you know what it is you will lose, it is often easier to make the choice. The acceptance is all.

We go to great lengths to maintain a status quo so that we do not have to lose anything, even to the point of repeating damaging behaviours. We are loath to activate this process ourselves, it always seems easier if someone takes something away from us. Then we can blame them.

Where there is a driving force for change, there usually exists a complementary force against it. Gestalt theorists describe this behaviour as resistance. It is not an absence of energy, but an energy that flows in a different direction. When resistance is consciously chosen, it is powerful and constructive. Contrary to Borg belief, resistance is not futile – it is energy and energy drives and moves things. It is inertia that keeps things the same. Staying the same means keeping things inert, or at least similar; and if you do what you have always done, you get what you have always got.

So when you choose a particular course of action, not only will you need to accept a loss, you can use the resistance as extra energy to move you on.

This leads us to the other fear that keeps us from choosing. Fear of hostility from others. If you believe the world is a hostile place, you don't believe you have a choice and end up protecting yourself against the hostile world. This is the fear of being disapproved of, of looking stupid, of getting it wrong.

Our attachment to people and things is what makes us fearful; fearful of losing them, usually by something we have done or are doing. When we feel we are losing them, we have a habit of making them 'bad', demonising them so that we feel better. When we are making decisions or choices, we often demonise other people, and make them responsible for our past, present and future.

We love to have leaders and bosses we can blame.

We develop cults of celebrity so that we can hold people up as icons and dash them down at the slightest trace of deviance from our illusion of perfection.

We can become victims and objects, enslaved by the demons we create.

Demonising others can be a fear of yourself, a fear of the power of your freedom.

Who would you hold up as an icon for you?

Who has had the most influence on your choices?

Who do you hold responsible for you?

When you answer those questions, think about whether you have held them responsible for anything in your life. Think about times when you have blamed others for your choices and decisions.

Time for a quick daydream...

So after that daydream, let's take a look at how fear of choice can play out in the world.

Three observations about the world in general:

No one is ever totally safe from harm.

Everyone is helpless when it comes to predicting what will happen next.

No one feels safe being completely open.

Three statements that you probably agree with, and yet you also probably struggle on a regular basis trying to protect yourself, predict what comes next, and feel scared to telling the truth.

It seems OK to know them but hard to accept them as a way of being.

Here is an illustration of how they played out in Jonathan's world.

Jonathan is a sufferer of KCS – King Canute Syndrome. He has a learned belief that he can control the world. (Yes, his data is very shaky on the truth of that, but who cares about data when you have the illusion of control.) He sits on his beach in Jonathanworld, and believes that he can control what goes on in the whole world. When you say this to him, he of course scoffs, and says "Well, I didn't mean the whole world, only my bit of it." Unfortunately, his bit of it is connected to the whole world. Pull on one piece of the world and you connect to another. This often sees Jonathan drowned on a regular basis.

Here is a map of how Jonathan sees the world:

His mental model and motto is "you can't control but you can have a bloody good go."

What he means by this is that his head logically tells him that he can't control everything, but his fear of failure means he believes he has to.

This results in a single focus for his world:

Do the right thing

Conditions for winning are:

It is impossible to fail: that is, it is unacceptable.

He has to know everything.

If one thing falls out of place, the whole plan fails.

There can be no deviation or change to his focus and plan.

Symptoms of this world:

Never relaxed;

Cannot enjoy anything;

Always doing;

Dislike of the new;

Yes, but…

Stuck in old patterns;

Staying in the light of the lamppost.

Outcomes of this world:

Jonathan sees the glass as half empty; nothing is ever good enough.

Frequent failure.

No sense of achievement even when things work out, as it was a 'foregone conclusion'.

Jonathan frequently cutting off his nose to spite his face.

No sense of freedom or choice.

A constantly frustrated Jonathan, who blames the world for his failure to control it.

No sign of keys.

How can Jonathan change his way of looking at the world?

There is one key that might change things dramatically for Jonathan. Because he only has a single outcome in his head, and feels the need to know everything, he is constantly confounded.

He needs to change his world view to at least a two-outcome scenario: he needs to want to do the right thing, but also be prepared to fail.

Being prepared to fail or lose means walking in the shadows.

Symptoms of a more-than-one-possibility world:
Acceptance of not knowing;
Acceptance of what he will lose;
Able to be confused;
Relaxed;
Yes, and...
Excited by newness.

Outcomes of this world:

The glass is half full.

Feeling in control by letting go.

More energy from using the resistance.

Less stress.

Sense of achievement as there was no foregone conclusion.

Knowledge gain and consequent growth.

The light comes from Jonathan's eyes, not the lamppost, so he can look where he pleases.

Can Jonathan make such a dramatic difficult shift? That is the $64,000 question. It is of course soooooo much easier to stick with what you know. If he can understand what he is doing, than at least he has a choice. Without that awareness, he is forced down his conditioned route.

However, it is the freedom to choose that we frequently avoid responsibility for.

What would you do?

PAUSE, even if it's brief. DON"T JUST READ ON. PUT THE BOOK DOWN AND THINK OF WHERE YOU ARE IN ALL OF THIS.

BE.

You don't really control anything.

Bruno Bettleheim describes what he calls the "ultimate freedom" of the prisoner in the concentration camp to choose his own attitude to his captors. This preservation of the inner right to revolt, even in this most extreme of circumstances where external result was not possible at all, made it possible in many cases for a person to survive. It was a central element in preventing psychological apathy, indifference and despair. (In those cases, people tended to wither away and die.) This inner capacity to choose your own attitude – to reserve the right to say NO even though you have done the specific thing you were asked to do – is what preserved a person's dignity as a human being.

You are free to do what you like. You need only face the consequences. As soon as you have thought of something, it is dead. Nothing survives being thought about. It becomes something quite different, and no longer the subject it was when you first thought about it. Dealing with fear means dealing with the feeling, not the thought that comes afterwards. That is the symptom.

So what would help you to make choices, and be with a fear of freedom?

You might have to read that a couple of times, but it does make sense eventually.

Coming back to the ability to know what it is you want, sometimes it is not because you don't know what you want, but that it is difficult to find words to describe it. So we sometimes find it easier to describe what we don't want, rather than what we do want.

Essential daydreaming

Take five minutes in your favourite chair, or the bath or shower, with a glass or mug of something you really like, put on your favourite music, or sit in silence, and let your thoughts wander. Let them wander and get yourself pictures of what you would really like to be doing, however crazy or unreal that is. (Sometimes it helps to set an alarm for five minutes, so that you are not worrying about how long you have had, or how much longer you have got.)

Let yourself be with the thoughts that matter to you. Just experience them. At the end of your five minutes, write down whatever comes into your head, no matter how unconnected, unrealistic or nonsensical it may sound.

The first time you do this it will probably feel weird and you will feel self-conscious.It may not, of course; indeed you may be doing it for much longer periods on a regular basis. However, doing this once a month keeps you grounded in *your* reality. Eventually, what emerges will be the feelings that are important to you. Then you can start thinking about what kind of environments or people would generate those kinds of feelings.

Starting to think about them means you need to be able to describe them.

Learning to describe is such a crucial weapon in being with fear. It is the opposite of judging which is a defence.

To tell someone that they are an 'Intuitive', which to them identifies all of their vague and unstructured behaviours; all of their loathing for detail, all of their joy and thinking on their feet, legitimises them. Defining yourself means you feel identified. Feeling identified means you feel that you belong somewhere. Feeling you belong somewhere makes you feel safe and wanted.

When you gather up experiences and situations, you discover that both you and others know them and recognise them, but because there is no word to describe them, they don't feel a real part of you.

So the vaguely uncomfortable feeling you got from sitting on a seat which is warm from somebody else's bottom is just as real a feeling as the one you get when a rogue giant elephant charges out of the bush at you, but hitherto only the latter had a word for it. Now they both have words. The first one is "Shoeburyness", and the second, of course, is fear.
DOUGLAS ADAMS

Trying to find words that describe your feelings and experience is half the battle. It is not only feelings that you need to learn to describe, it is also the ability to describe and interpret experience.

Try exploring decisions and choices you have made and what was behind them. Try and identify three things in each situation:

- Something that has identified both the strong and vulnerable sides to you in the situation.
- Something that links both the aspects of the situation and aspects of your character.
- Something that you have used to compensate for your defences; something that has exposed your true feelings rather than your strategies for hiding your feelings or defending against your fears.

SHADOWS Exercise

For five minutes, study the shadows of all the objects and people around you. Try to identify exactly which part of the object or person is casting a shadow.

For the next five minutes, continue to do this, but at the same time, focus on the problem you are trying to solve. Look for all the possible wrong solutions to the problem.

Finally, spend five more minutes studying the shadows and thinking about what correct solutions remain. Eliminate them, one by one, until only the single correct solution is left.

PAULO COELHO

Learning to describe and interpret you in situations helps to identify how your fears play out in reality. It allows you to see what triggers might arouse your defences, and begin to think how you might need to think in order to make choices with your fear rather than decisions that protect you against it.

Fear of choice is about the difference between the freedom of choice and the perceived data of a decision.

Being fearful of choice means that you might not know your keys even if you saw them.
Being fearful of choice means that you probably would not be sure about picking the keys up even if you found them.

Being with the fear means believing that there are keys.

It begins with taking the leap of faith to go into the shadows.
That has to be a choice, otherwise you won't be able to stay there.
Doing is a decision.
Being is a choice.
Being with your fear is a choice, not a decision.

Examine all paths with fear and then make your choice.

fear of choice

...Speak what we feel, not what we ought to say.
WILLIAM SHAKESPEARE, _King Lear_

*"I'm not strong enough to be as
vulnerable as you."*
CAREER GIRLS

fear of unworthiness

When I think my keys are in your shadow...

Fear of not being liked.
Fear of not being approved of.
Fear of not being valued.
Fear of looking stupid.
Fear of not being enough.

Big one this.

Have you ever felt pulled in so many directions that you didn't feel you could do anything right?

If you base your life around making other people happy, you will always be disappointed. Your desire is not only to make them happy but for them to like you as a result. If that is true, you are suffering from a fear of unworthiness; a fear of not being good enough. When you feel overwhelmed by a sense of unworthiness, you see the recognition of another person(s) as the only solution to your problem. This particular fear seems to be responsible for a large percentage of people's inability to be comfortable, courageous or candid.

By living a life that revolves around giving and getting, you are totally dependent on external validation for your growth. Whilst it undoubtedly helps to be valued and respected by others, if you do not possess the ability to do so intrinsically and validate yourself internally, you hand the helm of your life to someone else. Well, it does make life easier; if there is always someone to punish us or reward us, then nothing is ever our responsibility. We aren't responsible for our own keys, so we don't have to find them... So why are you still reading?

Provocation apart, the crazy thing about all this is that we usually know when we have screwed something up or done something well. And yet we carry with us a message from a long way back which says that in order to please others, we have to have them tell us we are a good or bad boy or girl. How does this play out in the real world?

A story of unworthiness...

ANTHONY WENT INTO HIS FATHER'S BUSINESS because he was the good boy. His sister had escaped from home at sixteen to his parents' unspoken dismay, but he had done what was expected of him, in a family where that didn't necessarily earn visible praise; but it didn't earn you disapproval.

Anthony was the Managing Partner in a large firm of accountants. Highly successful, he had clients who would only talk to him, allegedly, as well as managing the practice and doing its marketing and strategy. Too much for one person you would think; not Anthony. He felt that not taking on everything was tantamount to letting his father down. (His father had started the company, but had died several years before.) He developed a way of looking at the world where he was frightened of not being worthy, and could therefore nothing he did could ever be enough. He worked all hours, hardly saw his family, and said yes, he knew he was overdoing it to anyone who asked.

He felt that if he wasn't busy, he would not be approved of. He had built up a world where if he felt 'in control', that is doing everything that came onto his radar, he wouldn't have to face his fears. If, however, he were to stop doing it, he would have to face his presumptive fears of rejection and his dependence on others. He felt as though he would fall apart.

He felt so torn he metaphorically couldn't stand up. He had no personal centre of gravity with which he could focus himself from. All his energy and worth came from outside of him. By trying to make everyone happy he had made it impossible to either make them happy, or be happy himself. He found it impossible to prioritise, he was so scared of letting someone down, or not doing the right thing, that he ended up drowning in the trivia of voicemail and email.

What was he waiting for?

What was he frightened of?

Again, by keeping his defences up and trying to control his anxieties, he achieved what he was trying to avoid; people indeed thought him unworthy. He could not believe that he would ever be enough for anyone.

What would you say to Anthony?

If Anthony is going to be able to live his life at a pace that both he and his family will be able to tolerate, he needs to explore how he can be himself and what things are important to him, not figures from his past. He has started by wearing a T shirt around the house which says "I am enough."

Anthony's story will probably be familiar in parts to many of you. In reality, of course, there are people whom we want to please. How do we know what will please them, and when does it stop being something to make them happy, and become something that we define ourselves with?

So much of what we hold dear about ourselves arises from the expectation that we have of what other people are going to think of us – and our consequent fear of their disapproval. If you follow this line further, and ask what is it that their disapproval would bring, you often find, as in Anthony's case, a fear of rejection and subsequent abandonment.

A fear of being so unworthy that you would be left alone.

D. W. Winnicott, a British psychoanalyst, taught that to go willingly into the unknown was the key to living a full life. In order to do this, we need to develop the capacity to be alone. We cannot explore the world without the capacity to be alone in it.

We often suffer because of someone who doesn't love us, or someone who has left us, or someone who won't leave us. If we are alone, it is because no one wants us, if we are in a relationship, we transform it into a form of slavery.

The ability to be alone and feel safe is about learning to be yourself in the world and to feel that that in itself is enough. It means knowing:

When to do a job on your own.	*When to ask for help.*
When to hold on.	*When to let go.*
When to rely on others.	*When to rely on yourself.*

Do you know the differences for you?

Neither end of the axis is right or wrong. The question is whether it is the appropriate response to a situation.

Always being on one end of the axis means it is probably a defence. Defences keep you stuck in the same place. Not being able to be alone with your fear of unworthiness leaves you:

Stuck in the same pattern;
Stuck with the same results;
Stuck with the same frustration.

Sometimes the fear of alone is so great that we invite others in to make us feel better. So then we have given them a task that they may or may not be capable of. We also become dependent on them to feel safe. We have made our safety dependent on them. We have made our fear a reality. As well as that, if we are overly dependent on relationships with others, we only live in their experience; that means everything they need from the world and project onto it, including their fears.

You don't need theirs as well as yours.

If you are too worried by what other people think or what they might be doing, you lose *your* experience of being. By losing *your* experience, you lose you. This is that familiar feeling of not feeling enough, always feeling that there is something more you could or should be doing, a constant striving. That is extremely wearing, and has no positive outcome.

No wonder it makes us feel tired. Sometimes it just seems easier to find 'people like us', because then at least everyone else is as dissatisfied as we are, and misery loves company.

We often try to convince people to think as we do, because we believe that the more people there are who think like us, the more our truth will become more certain. We like people to support the same football team as us, like the same films and music, enjoy the same activities.

What is it about having this affirmation of ourselves that we are looking for? That if they think like me than they must approve of me. Phew. No rejection there.

When people look to find new relationships, it is their hobbies and tastes which attract. Of course it is much harder to ask what someone's politics are or their feelings about abortion might be. Even when those questions are asked, people seem unwilling to tell the truth for fear they might be rejected at first go.

As an illustration of this, a couple of years ago I was researching a book about relationships in the E-world, and I was looking at online dating agencies. What was fascinating to me was the huge reality gap between what people put on their personal profile, and what they really felt. For example, many people had written that how people looked was unimportant to them. My bullshit meter was on alert.

Interesting how many of those same people demanded a photo before they would meet up. The interest for me was not a judgement that they might be shallow; actually most humans have a physical and chemical response to one another. Why not admit it and say that your physiognomy does not light my fire? Fear of upsetting someone? That is the most common response, but when I asked people why they thought that that would be more upsetting than feeling revulsion and not telling, they could not give me an answer.

It reminded me of when I used to run workshops about giving bad news. I would tell people that there is no good way to deliver bad news, you just have to deliver it. Their response would be that's all very well, but if you are going to tell someone that they have B.O., they are going to be upset, so shouldn't you try to mitigate their pain? I think what they really meant was "do we have to tell them, can't we just leave deodorant in their desks?"

If you are recognising something that you have experienced here in these descriptions, start trying to get in touch with your fear.

What is it that you fear, when you have to deliver some bad news to someone, whether that news be that you don't love them any more, that they can't go out with their mates that night, or that they haven't got the promotion? My guess, from watching people for many years, is that you will say you are frightened that they will be upset. And why are you frightened of them being upset?

Ask yourself honestly and don't say because I don't want to upset them. That is a cop out, and doesn't answer the question. What is it about their being upset that would frighten you?

(Don't cop out by saying it doesn't frighten me. We associate 'frighten' with life and death things; but even when you say I am concerned or worried, what do you think that really means? It means that there is a reaction in the other person or the situation that you fear. Back to the question.)

For a lot of people, and you may be one of them or not, the honest response is that it would cause *you* pain, by seeing their hurt. It is that which you are avoiding. I could have told you a story about someone who that happened to, but I think I wanted to make the point that it is your fear of someone else's disapproval, or rejection that stops you being honest and clear.

This is why people fudge bad news by use of the immortal word 'but', or as the saying goes, everything before the but is bullshit.

I didn't mean to hurt you, I'm sorry that I made you cry...
WELL-KNOWN LIVERPUDLIAN SONGWRITER

Many films and songs have at their core the premise that I didn't mean it, I
didn't want to hurt you, so I...

- didn't tell you

- left you

- told you half-truths

We are so happy to see other people doing this, that we rejoice in someone
else having the same experience as us. Someone else has the same fear. Well, it
can't be all bad then... I'm not the only one who... I belong somewhere... I'm
not a reject. Logically, we know that not telling it like it is actually prolongs the
agony, but our fear of loathing is so strong that we can equally justify it.

Justification is a defence mechanism.
Do it and know you are doing it.
Know it for what it is. Fear of unworthiness.

Pause for a second and consider the times you have avoided giving bad news,
and run your story through this framework. Can you see yourself through it?

Pause for thought...

Question: Would people really reject you if you told them the truth?
How do you know?
Question your assumptions, ruthlessly.
If they did reject you, what would that mean for you?

So needing others' approval is dangerous for your own sense of self. If you depend on other people's approval, and need external validation, you are totally tied to them. You will feel powerless, because you have given them the power.

All these behaviours sound like a great way to waste your time. What might you be doing if you learned to feel enough?

You might feel:
comfortable with yourself;
happy with your achievements as they happen;
interested in others for themselves;
confident and relaxed.

Hmm. And you want to carry on not feeling enough because…?

Let me take a chance here and assume that you may be thinking 'so what should I be doing to try and think differently?' (If you aren't, don't read any further.)

One way to avoid this is not to reference yourself through others; on an extreme scale, that usually involves ascetic, hermit-like withdrawal. The power to be who and what you want to be lies in developing the awareness of when you need the support and guidance of others, and when you know the answers yourself. This information rarely comes in a flash of lightning; it usually takes many attempts and there are no rules. Expecting to know the right thing to do every time is going to lead to disappointment.

Relating to others is not the same as being dependent on them. A dependence on others to 'fix' you stops you creating momentum, because you have asked another to push you. That means they control your momentum. So it isn't about depending on them, it is about *learning to relate to them.* That means not needing something for you (that is wanting to please so that they reward you with their approval) from every interaction. (Read that sentence again.)

The inner power has far less to do with pleasing the powerful or impressing the powerless than it does with doing as I please. It depends more on experiencing my input than on displaying my output.

SHELDON KOPP

A need to display your output comes from a fear of disapproval from others, a fear that you will not be approved of. Inner power has little to do with the trappings of power. At the same time that you seek to feel more powerful in yourself, you give other people the power to control your life by a need for recognition. We hold ourselves back from doing things for fear they may not meet with approval.

And therefore what?

The 'so what' might be that you:

> miss out on what you really wanted
> feel regret and worry and feel stressed about it afterwards
> incur others disapproval for doing nothing

Still sound like a good idea?

Paul was so scared of his partner rejecting him that he proposed to her as she was falling asleep in bed. He said "Will you marry me?" as she was half asleep. This was his fifth attempt at proposing; he had decided to do it on her birthday, on holiday and on various other occasions, but the words would not come into his mouth.

Even when she had said yes, he was still frightened of rejection by his family. He went home to his parents and was so frightened of his family being there that he became totally lost for words. He was so scared that they would disapprove he lost the power of speech and even the ability to work out what he wanted to say.

Sounds crazy to you, maybe, but not to Paul.

Thinking the unthinkable; making mistakes: these are things that **increase**, not decrease, personal power.

We can only do them if we believe we are enough; we are worthy...

Under pressure there are times when we discover that our belief in ourselves is more fragile than we wish. By the same token some situations can surprise us and allow us to see how much influence we really have. If you want more control over yourself, you only get it by stopping the desire to control or be approved of by others. You need to learn to be enough. If you do this, you are far less likely to experience this feeling of helplessness. When we try to control others, we are most at risk of being exploited by them.

Domination and submission are not necessarily determined by one person being stronger than the other. It's all in the perception. In situations where people have equal power, the one who lets the other get away with defining the relationship is likely to end up feeling oppressed.

High status/low status... The raised eyebrow or superior tone of voice suggest that you would have to be mad or stupid to disagree. If you accept this threat of course you will feel dominated. Sometimes we are the ones putting out the behaviour; the raised eyebrow, the superior tone of voice. We do this so that others will obey us (and in doing so, of course, respect and honour us).

Sheldon Kopp suggests that you sometimes try to indulge your need for omnipotence, and try telling the person that what you really want is to have everything your own way all of the time. Interesting exercise...

When we feel the lack of control, we often make our fear of unworthiness come true by being turbo-unworthy. So sometimes we either try hard to point the finger out there somewhere and make it their responsibility, or we turn on ourselves and say we were really, really unworthy. Feeling unworthy or powerless can exaggerate people's characters by pushing their personal style to extremes. For example, some become so humbled by their helplessness that they become constantly passive and unassuming. This is the low-status position. The ultimate expression of low status is where we act so dumb about doing something that people get to do things for us, to protect and take care of us. (Well at least they don't abandon us and leave us alone.)

Learned helplessness is a state where we learn to be helpless so that we either get other people to do things for us or we demonise others into being so awful that we can say "see, I told you life was awful and that would happen". Others are so full of the anger of their impotence that they live their lives in a state of chronic irritability (Victor Meldrew, perhaps).

Sometimes we over idolize, perhaps to make us even more unworthy.

All this to stay in the lamplight.

All this to not go into the shadows and feel the fear of not being enough.   *Hmm...*
All this for what may well be something we have created, and of which others
are completely unaware.

Has anyone ever said to you " I just wanted your feedback..." or "I just wanted you to say that you loved me..."?

Has your response ever been "Well, why didn't you ask?"

Have you ever asked? I mean have you ever checked out your assumption that people see you as unworthy, or not good enough?

Despite our need for others to think like us in a paradoxical way we rarely think they do, because if we did think that we would know that they don't often see us in a hostile way and were not withholding from us. (I know they might be sometimes, but not *every* time...)

So are you keeping them in a position where even if they said you were worthy, you wouldn't say thank you, you would be so uncomfortable with a change in position?

Do you want to stay unworthy?

No, seriously, would you want to change to those states I described before of happiness, confidence, etc.?

You know what I am going to ask next... So what keeps you unworthy?

What would you have to be feeling to feel enough?

Logically, it can't be from anyone else.

You have to feel enough YOURSELF.

How can you create the space for yourself when you are used to someone creating it for you? How can you make the rewards intrinsic as opposed to extrinsic?

First you have to lose the fear of displeasing others, or at least lose its importance to you.

So by now you know that stage one is accepting the fear.

Accepting that you define yourself through the approval of others.

Accepting that you are worried about being 'good enough'.

Accepting means knowing you are doing, thinking or feeling something, and are responsible for the impact of that thought or feeling.

OK, let me sneak in a little doing here after all this being and accepting. How do we recognise actions, feelings and thoughts as unworthy?

One thing to help do that would be to label the thought. By labeling it, we are admitting its existence and therefore allowing ourselves to do something with it. Labeling might look like "having a thought: she is very bossy" or "having a thought: he is being unfair to me." If the thoughts are tumbling out so fast that you can't recognise anything except confusion, label the mess "confusion". If you take away the belief that you have been wronged, and with it goes the feeling. If you take away the feeling that you have been injured or hurt, the injury and hurt disappears.

Even an acceptance in this way is very liberating; you no longer have the need to spend tremendous amounts of energy holding something back, or concealing it. By surfacing it and speaking it, you can also get a perspective on it – whether it is something that is worthy of your attention, and is really fearful, or whether it isn't worth holding on to, and you can let it go. "She is impossible" and "having a thought: she is impossible" are two very different ways of looking at the world. One judges and makes the problem external, the other owns a thought and makes it a thought, not a judgement.

How we see others is a huge key to the traps we set for ourselves. By casting another in a 'higher status' role to us, we automatically hand over control. In doing that we give away our responsibility and accountability. Makes life much easier. So unless the other person happens to want to let you do what you would rather be doing, you don't get to do it. But then you do have someone to blame. Whereas if you take the chance and the risk yourself, you may not be prepared to take the failure. Taking a risk means taking the possibility of failure. It is not a risk without that possibility. Many a time in life we say we are taking a risk, but are not taking the on the risk of failure, and are devastated when things don't work out.

Change how you perceive the things or people you are trying not to be fearful of.

Even your actions can denote status: we hold eye contact when we want to dominate someone, or when we look at someone we admire, but we break eye contact and take quick glances when we are feeling submissive. We try to please 'higher status' people by ruining our posture, and constricting our voices. Usually the person who is playing the higher status takes up the most space.

If you touch your mouth when you look at someone, you'll feel hesitant but will be perceived as 'lowering' your status. If you hold your head still, people perceive 'high' status. If you're aware that you are keeping your head still, it actually makes you feel in control. (Try saying "Make my day" while moving your head around – it doesn't have quite the same effect.)

Even when we have experienced the power of letting go, and know what we can do, it is sometimes easy to keep ourselves in known situations. So we choose 'audiences' we are comfortable with, people who won't disapprove. When something goes wrong we blame situations or people who have intruded onto our 'stage'.

The novice freezes, the more experienced person goes to a sophisticated series of defence mechanisms. Neither wants to change or lose what they perceive to be control.

Improvisation theatre is an interesting place to look for patterns of behaviour, because being a good improviser means letting go, being in the moment and accepting what is happening around you and responding directly to it, not to preconceived notions of your own. They describe four key groups of defences:

BLOCKING
This defence is about staying the same, not being changed, maintaining the illusion of control, not being hit by the bus. You also minimise the transitions you may have to make by being negative.

Sound familiar?   Yes, but...

CANCELLING
When in this mode, you dismantle whatever has been established. Nothing has been or can be achieved. You don't respond to others, you ignore both them and any suggestions they make. You might withhold information or not add to ideas.

Sound familiar? What did you say?

SIDETRACKING

This avoids interaction by talking about things that are happening elsewhere or at another time. Change the subject, make a joke, gossip, waffle, be 'clever', take the attention away from the situation, either to you or something else.

Sound familiar? Did you want some coffee? Well I knew someone who...

DRIVING

Take control by setting clear direction for everyone else, and tell them what the story is. You are no longer relative to the people around you.

Sound familiar? What I think you should do is....

These are all reactions to a fear of disapproval. Stopping this is all dependent on your awareness of your fear.

One way to raise awareness is to write down all your mistakes over the last month (or year or week or day), or have someone do it for you. Then ask yourself to make the mistakes deliberately.

Another way is to forbid yourself to do the very thing you know you have to do but feel you can't. It is astonishing how quickly forbidden fruit becomes attractive; and if *you* break the rules, it's your choice and your power.

Telling people who are afraid to touch each other that they are now forbidden to do so allows the excitement to overcome the fear.

Telling someone who has procrastinated over something that their time is up and they can no longer do what they were supposed to do seems to stir them into action.(It doesn't always work, but it's got to be worth a try.)

OK, enough doing, let's get back to being.

The key to these rather contrary behaviours is accepting the fear. It is fear that creates all the stuck behaviours. Fear of not being accepted, approved of, valued. Knowing what the fear is about helps an enormous amount, but doesn't take the fear away.

You don't need to take the fear away. Experiencing the fear and changing your reaction to it lessens the potential damage the fear can do. If you live in a world where you are not in constant need of external validation, the external world has all the power. It can only have it if you give it. It can't take it from you.

Accepting the fear means YOU hold on to the power.
When you deal with fear, the way out is in.
So try naming your thoughts feelings and actions, and being more observant of you in relation to others.

I know it is only a start, but that really is all a book can give you; a place to start, some understanding of how things might happen, and some things to be aware of. You have to be aware to start.
Not an answer. A starting point.

So start.

You can of course get so lost in the observation and analysis that you lose the experience and meaning. Chris's story is a story of an individual who was beginning to come to terms with a fear of unworthiness that he masked with his extraordinary thinking powers. He knew with his head, but not deep down.

You can only find truth with logic if you have already found truth without it.
G.K. CHESTERTON

Chris felt that he had to be capable at all times, that nothing could ever be out of control in his life. He had always been regarded as the 'best' and 'most talented'. One of the first things he described was the fact he remembered at an early age scoring 149 on an intelligence test. That made him one point below genius. That's quite a story to be living with. He never had it tested again, for fear that he would not have improved, but spent most of his adolescent and adult life being the 'boy genius', always feeling the need to outperform and outthink others. He had grown up very fast, and indeed had coped admirably with extremely demanding parents, but he had grown on an insecure foundation and a denial of what he wanted to be in the world. His fear of not being approved of by other people, whether personal or professional, meant that he was always 'on', and always had to be thinking and ready for what might come next.

At an early age he had lost touch with his ability to put himself on pause. He could do it when he employed analytical techniques and methodologies, but it was an artificial pause, and one which involved his head, not all of him. His actions were based on what he deemed necessary to survive and be recognised and loved – a boy wonder. He was overly reliant on his ability to work everything out, but when something irrational came up, particularly if it related to feelings, he would escape into analysis. Whenever it felt to him that this control was threatened – a project not running to time, not being able to hit his required pace when running, his wife's moods, he became depressed.

When I commented on this behaviour, he immediately began to analyse it. It was almost as if he wished to be powerless, but did not know how. It seemed that he lacked to capacity to be, and had not learned that he had to ride the waves of the things he could not control, not go down under them. He felt imprisoned by the very actions that he felt had protected him; indeed they probably had. They were probably suitable for a time in the world he inhabited as a child. They were not suitable for the world he inhabited as an adult, and indeed were not even protecting him; instead, they were crushing him.

He turned everything he experienced into something he did, instead of sometimes letting it be something he was.

Eventually his body had enough and decided that if he would not let his head feel something, then the body would respond in a way that he could not ignore. He became unable to sleep, experienced heavy night sweats and found it difficult to talk coherently. He found himself standing in all sorts of positions which only served to exacerbate the stress he was already feeling.

Chris's body was saying 'shut up and be'. He was forced to take time out from work. It was actually the only way he could break the patterns he had set up for himself. He had to allow himself to be silenced. Even when he first started to

Most feeling states are experienced primarily in the body, so an awareness of your body really helps to connect with your feelings. Repressing the expression of strong emotions appears to exaggerate the intensity of the physiology that goes with them.

recover from his physical signs, almost his first words "were what do I do now?" He set about getting himself back to work at the same level he was before his crisis. He still was having difficulty being with himself. His new fear was not only the old one, (because he had never really accepted it), but now a new one, which was a fear of not being able to get back to the respected position he had had.

After a period of recovery and even getting back to work and receiving the approval he sought, he found himself suffering from the night sweats and mood swings again.

What he had tried to do was solve a problem by thinking about it, working it out. This led to all kinds of theories, but no improvement. Again, he had no real idea about what he was feeling, and remarkably little idea of the difference between a feeling and a thought.

Two major changes came to pass as a result of this 'second coming':

■ he started to take notice of his body and learned to breathe in and out of difficult feeling states.

■ He had to discover a whole new vocabulary for his emotions.

He had felt the unpleasant physical sensations and the mounting internal frustration. He began to experience that emotions, however powerful, are not overwhelming if they are acknowledged and given room to breathe. He needed help to translate those feelings into something he felt about himself and his situation.

Learning to interpret and translate emotion into words does not come easily, and first you need to become able to detach the influence of the past from your being in the present. The person you were then had legitimate feelings and responses; that does not mean you as you are now has to have the same ones. You have had more experiences that have shaped you, and are no longer in the same position as the younger person whose memories you carry.

Learning to substitute the need for external approval by internal approval from himself is probably the most difficult part of his change process.

This began for Chris by cutting himself some slack and not pressurising himself to 'perform'.

That made him proud of himself for the first time in his life.

Separating that need for approval from others in the past to the need for approval in the here and now (intrinsic or extrinsic), is crucial to the ability to see in the shadows.

Hilary Austen, a learning and communications analyst, suggests that looking behind the behaviours to the patterns and themes helps us work out a principle for dealing with them. A principle does not have the obsessive, compulsive, stifling qualities of a ritual. It is a way of being that is actionable, portable, personalisable and revisable.

This means it is:

Portable	*something that can be transferred from situation to situation.*
Revisable	*something that can be upgraded and adapted to new situations.*
Personalisable	*something that fit your own character, and doesn't belong to anyone else.*
Actionable	*something that achieves a difference and connects to something concrete.*

The stuckness can provide us with a way out. Acknowledging the traps and where they come from allows us to adapt the knowledge to another outcome other than being stuck. At that point you can have a choice. First you have to admit you are stuck. No, really admit it, not 'Yes, but...' Then try these principles as a framework for designing your way out; they are not a solution, just a way to help you think about what you need to think about.

It is about self. Your self is constructed by YOU for YOU. You construct that self, usually in response to circumstances and the actions or words of others. You construct the darkness and the shadows. The lamppost doesn't do it.

YOU DO.

If you can believe it, than you can logically believe that YOU can change the construction of your self, certainly the bit that responds to others.

Think about that for a second, or maybe even a minute.

Why would you do that? Well, you may want to feel more power over what you achieve, more confident, more content: whatever. Your motive has to be good enough for you to try, and where you are now has to feel uncomfortable enough for you to want to move off it.

This is about changing your mental model of you in the world. It is not just about changing the way you behave with and towards others, or even changing what is behind your actions towards them. It is more fundamental. It is about changing your whole way of being with others.

It is about relating to them, not depending on them.

This is a totally different way of defining you, how you work, and what you are about. This is about a you that has gone from being made up of various themes and roles relating to others, to a you who is aware of your relationship to others, and sees yourself as **subject**, rather than *object* to them.

It is about your confidence in yourself, not their confidence in you.

You create the light and the shadows. Not the lamppost.
Now can you see the keys?

of unworthiness

fear

"Hope is an orientation of the spirit, an orientation of the heart; it transcends the world that is immediately experienced and is anchored somewhere beyond its horizons.

Hope is definitely not the same thing as optimism. It is not the conviction that something will turn out well, but the certainty that something makes sense, regardless of how it turns out.

In short, I think that the deepest and most important form of hope is something we get from elsewhere. It is also this hope, above all, which gives us the strength to live and continously try new things."

VACLAV HAVEL, _Disturbing the Peace_

The end is important in all things

GHOST DOG

fear of ending

YOU AND YOUR SHADOWS

The range of what we think and do
is limited by what we fail to notice.
And because we fail to notice
that we fail to notice
there is little we can do
to change until we notice
how failing to notice
shapes our thoughts and deeds.
R.D. LAING

Fear of ending.

Fear of ending is about acknowledging what you are about to lose or may indeed have already lost.

Fear of ending is about fear of beginning.

Yup, it's a circle.

Fear of beginning is about accepting loss and accepting the unfamiliarity and confusion of the new.

So how do you start an ending?
Not without a beginning, and not without an awareness of a need for an ending.

Every new beginning comes from some other beginning's end.
SEMISONIC

Finishing a book like this generally leaves people full of questions, and with a sense of "What now?" Well, it's a bit like that for this writer too. I would love to be there to ask you questions about what the book has raised for you; to help you explore unknown territory, to be uncomfortable. But I can't.

So what can I say that might be of value right now?
I suppose it's mainly admonitions; advice to the fearful.

OK, so first of all...

Try not to overreact.

Every twinge of dysfunction in our bodies is not necessarily the manifestation
of a deep-seated fear, or a manifestation of a stress-related disease. The real
world is full of bad things that we can keep at bay by altering the way we think
and psychological makeup. The world is also full of awful things that cannot be
eliminated by a change of attitude, no matter how sincerely, fervently and
heroically we may wish. Understanding the difference between the two is part
of the GREAT KEY HUNT.

Curiosity, flexibility and resilience are really helpful mindsets to have in order
to know what can and cannot be changed. As Reinhold Niebuhr said, it takes
wisdom, courage and acceptance to distinguish between the things you can
and can't change. The unpredictable world needs no constructions to manage
it. It will always be unpredictable.

Opportunities are always happening. You just don't see them if you are not
paying attention.
F8 and be there.

Secondly...

The universe is not safe, you cannot control it.

Safety is static, and therefore incompatible with life and change.
You can hide and you can run, but you can't do both at the same time.

If you are not under the illusion of being in control through defence
mechanisms, you know that there is no way to avoid feeling vulnerable;
no way to avoid feeling angry or hurt;
no way to be sure that you will be accepted.
It might not be what you thought it would be, but it would BE (real).

Get used to disappointment.
WILLIAM GOLDMAN

Thirdly...

Don't look to actions for reward;
look to new ways of thinking and being.

If you divorce peace from chaos, it sterilises and fixates the very actions you intend to be free of. Maybe even a desire for peace is a desire to control the universe and life, but there is something about the cycles of life and the necessity and time for all things, including fear.

Don't force yourself into a contest between will power and won't power.
It isn't discipline, a schedule or an action plan that will help.
Trying to ignore the problem, hoping it will disappear by itself, usually works for a short while. Then it reappears, sometimes in a more dramatic form.
Trying to figure out the problem usually leads to all kinds of theories, but no improvement.
It's changing the way you think about things.

Fourthly...

Accept and welcome mistakes. Don't be distracted by perfection.

Being efficient and effective does not mean you have to be perfect. It is the need for perfection that creates the stress and fear, and ultimately destroys the ability to enjoy, be and live.

Robert Altman suggests that all the high points in his films come from mistakes; not errors that were written in, but from an environment where there is room for them to occur and be used. The creativity is in the letting go. So you can rehearse and be prepared, and also allow the mistake to happen. The search for relief from stress, happiness or fulfillment is a personal one and not a model we can pass on to others. You have to know what you seek and what you fear. Salmon jump over waterfalls, giving themselves up to the water, but knowing where they want to go. Even when people experience it, many cannot accept their own victory or power. They give up their dreams when they know they can be realised. They are only of value if you know what you want to do with them.

Someone else telling you the answer only demonstrates that it is possible. Learning means making it your own, and possible for yourself. Allow yourself to experience the fear, and the simplicity of the response is amazing. Sometimes when the going gets tough, we have a desire to give up the fight because we define it as not being worth the effort. We are often prisoners of the past, in that we don't do things because previously we failed at them, and so we may fail again. You even become afraid that achievements made might be lost if you fail at something else. We need an incentive to do anything with commitment, but in terms of personal growth, being at peace with ourselves, being more of ourselves, whatever it is we have chosen to seek, there are no guarantees. Even when we are close we are perfectly capable of self-destruction. One step from success is where one's strength begins to flag; it is easy to lose confidence in yourself and drown in a sea of regret. At our most difficult moment, we fear failure and want to give up before it happens.

At that moment you need to stop anticipating and be.

The greatest source of strength we have is our present; what we are doing NOW. That is where the will to win and the enthusiasm and power lies.

Fifthly, and lastly...

There is no cure for fear.

You don't want a cure for fear. It is not a disease, it is a part of you, and as such you can make it more or less prominent in your life. Any cure implies some kind of perfection and infallibility.

Being fallible is part of being.
It puts the fear into context.

Accepting and engaging fear is the only way to change anything about yourself. You can't protect yourself from fear by distancing yourself from it.

By now you may be asking yourself many questions about how you respond in different situations. (If you are not, why not?)

Don't be afraid to re-read things. Go back and look at the things that mattered to you on first reading. Ask more questions. Observe yourself more. Be aware of other people's reactions to you. Check your understanding. Keep on checking your assumptions. Once you have the information about yourself, you have a choice about what options and choices are available to you.

If you have troubled to get this information, and don't use it, then you are probably trying very, very hard not to.

So if it's the unpredictability that worries you, know yourself well enough to at least anticipate; you may be able to recognise signals and therefore respond better. A person without knowledge is always a half a second away from the next pain.

You might even see the keys....

I know you aren't supposed to do this in an ending chapter, but it's hard to know where to go next, so here is another metaphor that may help. You can always ignore it.

To help understand some of the difficulty in moving forward, let me give you a metaphor from Gestalt therapy. Gestalt is a way of experiencing the feelings you have in the moment. One Gestalt exercise involves trying to have the difficult conversations that have previously proved impossible. The therapist places two chairs in a room and asks the client to talk to the chair as if they are the person they wish to have the conversation with. The client talks to the chair and says what they want to say; they then sit in the chair and respond as that person might. Having the conversation in this way seems to enable people to say things they could not say before, and see things from a different perspective.

K. T. Miller suggests you need a third chair. When in the third chair, the client describes how they might feel after they have had the conversation.

The first two chair positions are like the realisation and the naming of what it is that troubles you and others. The third chair is about what might happen next. The third chair is very hard to move into, because quite often we have so much invested in the first and second chairs that it's hard to give it up and move to an unknown quantity, even though we may think it's the right thing to do.

What would it be like to sit in that chair?
What would you say?

Sitting in the third chair requires possession of the keys. You can't sit there unless you have been in the other two chairs.
So somewhere in the shadows is the third chair. When you are sitting in it, the light doesn't come from the lamppost; it comes from you. You create the light. You don't need the artificial external help of the lamppost. You have it.
Mix those metaphors...

Feeling more productive, less stressed, more energized, comes with your adjustment to being in the dark. The more you know yourself and accept yourself, the easier it gets to go into the shadows and find your keys.

Keep asking the questions, the more you stand in the shadows, the more your eyes get accustomed to them and the more you will see.

The more you can see, the more comfortable you will be with your presence in the shadows.

of ending *fear*

Live so that you don't look back and regret that
you've wasted your life.
Live so you don't regret the things you have
done or wish that you had acted differently.
Live life honestly and fully
Live.

ELISABETH KUBLER-ROSS

The keys are in the dark. Go there.

RECIPE FOR HAPPINESS IN KHABAROVSK OR ANYPLACE

One grand boulevard with trees
With one grand café in sun
With strong black coffee in very small cups

One not necessarily very beautiful
man or woman who loves you

One fine day
LAURENCE FERLINGHETTI

things to help you when you're on keys expeditions

Things to consider and do when you're standing in the shadows

KEY POINTS

■ It's not the feeling of fear that inhibits growth; it's the way you respond to the feeling that renders it constructive or destructive. YOU choose.

■ The more you defend against a fear, the bigger it becomes, and your perceived need to defend against it.

■ Trying to control an irrational feeling such as fear by using rational thought is like trying to put out a fire with oil (totally irrational).

■ Fear and desire are so closely linked that when you defend against one you inevitably defend against the other, and therefore defend yourself from the truth you are.

Being in touch with fear generates tension and anxiety. Bearing in mind that finding your keys involves *responding*, not reacting, to fear, we still have to know what that anxiety may produce. When we receive something that we perceive to be painful, our bodies generate a physiological stress response (e.g., the heart rate goes up and hormones such as glucocorticoids and adrenaline are secreted). If these responses become regular we can do long-term damage to ourselves, not just in terms of cardio-vascular problems but with memory, depression. If we can find a way to respond to those painful stimuli and not just react to them, the potential damage is greatly diminished. We deal better with frustration when we have outlets; when we punch a cushion, play tennis, take a run. Sometimes just imagining those outlets can have a beneficial effect. (It can increase the frustration when you appreciate that something is stopping you doing them; you have to accept that they are imaginary.)

So consider what works for you when you need to displace the frustration. Believe it or not, there is ample research to show that when confronted with stress, most humans decrease their responses when surrounded by other humans that they like and/or respect. They then choose to talk, hold or cry with those people, decreasing the negative physiological fear responses. Even if you are someone who feels better when the reverse is true – that is, when you are truly on your own – and you can either be in silence, turn the music up very loud, watch a film or even talk to someone on the telephone. (There are no absolute rules here about what works every time, as most people in situations can be both the appeaser and the source of the fear inducer – e.g. families, relationships, work itself… it is situational.)

In short, not only know your fears, also know what responses allow you to be with them.

With or without people?

Doing something or not doing something?

Quiet or noisy?

Etc…

Recognise it, put yourself on pause, feel it, then explore it.

The Speed Exercise

Walk for twenty minutes at half the speed at which you normally walk. Pay attention to the details, people, and surroundings. The best time to do this is after lunch.

Repeat the exercise for seven days.

It is we who define the speed at which we do things. It is we who determine how quickly time passes.

Sometimes changing the way you do routine things allows a new person to grow.

In memory of Douglas Adams.

Name some of the situations or experiences you have had that provoked feelings that you have but you don't have words to describe. If you are feeling particularly creative, name them after a place anywhere in the world that somehow (however irrational), most closely represents the feeling.

(For example, that feeling you have when you go into the kitchen, or indeed any other room, wondering what you went in there for, Douglas Adams refers to as "Woking".)

Jed's limber

Think about five key emotional situations in your life. Choose one, then try to bring back the visceral sense of the emotion(s) involved. (Perhaps an object, photograph, song, may help). Imagine and visualise an entirely fictional film scene in your mind that captures and conveys that emotion as fully as possible. Think on terms of images, sounds and character behaviour, but don't worry about the plot or surroundings. Focus on the emotion as expressed in terms of light, body language, dialogue, behaviour, etc. (If you want to stretch yourself, try writing it out. Don't explain, just tell us what we would see and hear.)

Adapted from Jed Dannenbaum

Difficult questions:

What's the big problem (describe in every detail)?

Where is this problem 'real'?

What's the stance hidden within this problem?

How do you contribute to the creation of this problem?

What do you get out of this problem being as it is?

How do you keep your stance hidden?

Why do you keep your stance hidden?

What conditions would need to be present for you to change/under what circumstances?

What would make you change?

David Firth, *Freedom and Power*

Being Zorba

"A man needs a little madness or else he never dares cut the rope."

Zorba the Greek
(I daresay he meant to include women in that statement.)

What would your madness be?
What would make you really really laugh uncontrollably?
What would make you really really cry uncontrollably?

"When a man is full, what can he do? Burst."

Zorba the Greek

Burst forth in the shadows.
I dare you.

"Anything that happens, happens."

D.N. ADAMS